WRITE ON!

WRITE ON!
Business Writing Basics

Jane Watson

Self-Counsel Press
(*a division of*)
International Self-Counsel Press Ltd.

Printed in Canada

First edition: March 1996; Reprinted: December, 1996

Canadian Cataloguing in Publication Data
    Watson, Jane, 1948-
    Write on!

    (Self-counsel business series)
    Includes bibliographical references
    ISBN 1-55180-027-6

    1. Business writing. 2. English language — Business English.
    3. Business communication. I. Title. II. Series.
    HF5718.3.W37 1996   808'.066651   C96-910025-6

Cover photography by Terry Guscott, ATN Visuals, Vancouver, B.C.

Cover props courtesy of Willson Stationers

Self-Counsel Press
(*a division of*)
International Self-Counsel Press Ltd.

1481 Charlotte Road	1704 N. State Street
North Vancouver, British Columbia	Bellingham, Washington
V7J 1H1	98225

This book is dedicated to my best friend and husband, Colin, to my wonderful support staff, to my children — John, Timothy, and Suzanne — and to my mother, Mary Thomas.

Special thanks also goes to my mentor Warren Evans and business colleagues and friends.

CONTENTS

SAMPLES

WORKSHEETS

TABLES

CHECKLISTS

PREFACE

During my school years, I never excelled at putting my thoughts on paper. True, occasionally I received an "A" and some praise from a teacher, but for the most part I was content to be an average student in preparing essays and reports.

Then I entered the workforce as an office manager for a government department. Shortly thereafter, the department was merged with another, and there were several women on staff much more qualified to run an office than I. My new employer decided that as I was a university graduate who couldn't type, the best place for me would be the writer's pool. In those days, writers all had antiquated typewriters on which they would hunt and peck their stories with two fingers, cut and paste the material together — with real scissors and glue — and turn it over to a professional typist to prepare.

I was extremely fortunate. The *Toronto Telegram* newspaper had recently folded, and some of the reporters had been hired by the ministry to write speeches, reports, audio-visual scripts, brochures, and news releases. I found myself working with four highly experienced writers who delighted in telling me how to improve my writing. One of my "editors" was Bill Dodds, who later became a good friend and mentor. Bill never accepted an "adequate" article, and he forced me to write and rewrite until I learned to drop the stilted style of the academic world and write the facts clearly and directly.

After several years under Bill's wing, I left the government and stayed home with my young children, teaching part time at the local community college. My subjects, of course, were business writing and correspondence and report writing.

As the children grew older, I started my own training and consulting company in the field of business communications. For the past decade I have been a professional speaker in the field of business communications and have conducted countless in-house and public workshops in writing skills, written numerous articles on communications, and appeared on radio and TV. I also provide a one-on-one mentoring program for senior managers.

One of my favorite quotations is "Find what you enjoy doing, and you'll never work a day in your life." I have been blessed in discovering what I truly enjoy doing — assisting others to improve their communications skills.

Writing this book was a challenge. It involved collecting and answering all the questions I have been asked about writing and putting the answers on paper, as well as relaying the most useful tricks I have learned over the years.

I wanted *Write On!* to be three things —

(a) a practical guide for business people, whether they are working for themselves or someone else,

(b) as up-to-date as possible for today's marketplace, and

(c) easy to read.

For this reason, I organized the material into short points or rules. Readers can pick up the book, turn to any page, and read a point that can be immediately incorporated into their normal business correspondence. All of the points are useful; incorporating even a few into your writing will make a difference.

Best wishes and happy writing!

1

BUSINESS WRITING — THERE HAVE BEEN SOME CHANGES MADE

Whenever I conduct a business writing workshop — whether it is for the general public or a customized in-house session — there are always a few people in the audience who are upset by, or strongly object to, the idea that they should update their writing styles.

When told that effective business writing calls for simple words matching their readers' vocabulary level, they complain that the English language is being "watered down."

When it is explained that today's writing should be more direct and less formal than it was a decade ago, they disagree. Clichés are fine, they claim. After all, the style that suited their parents and teachers should be good enough today.

However, these people are ignoring the fact that lifestyles, business practices, and technology have changed. Typewriters, personal secretaries knowledgeable in grammar, shorthand, dictionaries on desks, photocopiers, fax machines, office computers, unit secretaries, personal computers, laptops, spell checkers, grammar checkers, e-mail, the Internet.

These are only a few of the new resources that had an impact on writing styles.

From the early 1920s to the 1970s, a manager would dictate a letter to his or her secretary, who would type it and send it out. The letter would be written in a verbose style aimed at impressing the reader with the sender's education and literary style. And because a third party was involved — the secretary — it tended to be rather impersonal.

Then, in the early 1980s, we were hit by a recession. North American business strategies changed and companies became leaner and more streamlined. Readers wanted their correspondence to match. They no longer wanted to take the time to sort through wordy, stilted messages and irrelevant details. They were focused on "the facts, just the facts."

This demand was further reinforced by the amount of paper crossing readers' desks. By 1992, business people received at least six times as much reading material — letters, memos, reports, faxes — as they did in 1982. Today's readers don't have the time to absorb convoluted messages. They want to read a message just once and know precisely what they should do next. Sentences such as "Kindly execute the attached documents and return them at your earliest convenience to the undersigned at the above address," are no longer appropriate. They are too vague and have the reader's eyes roving all over the page to pick up the details.

A key idea to remember is that, previously, writers wrote about their interests or what they wanted the reader to know. However, an experienced communicator today writes about what the reader *needs* to know.

TONE

This brings us to tone, or how the message is delivered. In the past, writers used very formal words and phrases. This was the normal language of the day. People tended to — and were expected to — speak formally. If you use these same words and tone in talking with a client or customer today, you are regarded as old-fashioned and pompous.

The same is true for your writing. Whether you are communicating internally with staff or externally with customers, you should write in a friendly, courteous fashion, using the same words and tone you would use if you were meeting the reader face to face.

Tell the reader what you can do, rather than what you can't. If you are listing features, include benefits. Use the active voice. Include the reader's name. And use words that are common to your normal conversation. For example, I doubt if any human resources person would ever say, "A prompt reply will expedite consideration of the student's application." If you wouldn't say it, don't write it.

Today, write as though you are speaking — assuming you speak in a grammatically correct fashion. And that brings us to the next point: grammar.

GRAMMAR*

Grammar is making a comeback. In the past, many managers depended on their secretaries to correct their spelling and punctuation errors. However, due to down sizing, right sizing, and re-engineering, personal secretaries are becoming rare. For the most part, white-collar workers are now expected to use computers to input, revise, and edit their own correspondence and reports.

Surprisingly, this hasn't led to an increase in ungrammatical writing. Individuals are now paying more attention to their own correspondence. And more and more executives

---

*Unfortunately, there is not enough room in this book to include all the important grammar rules as well as the necessary style rules. For an excellent reference book on grammar, I recommend *Write Right!* by Jan Venolia.

are requesting grammar workshops, reference books, or software programs to improve their accuracy.

One of the best ways you can ensure that your grammar is correct is to keep a comprehensive, recently published grammar book handy. (Throw out any books more than five years old.) Then, read everything that crosses your path with a critical eye. If a sentence is punctuated in an unusual fashion, don't accept it as accurate. Check it out.

COMPUTER SOFTWARE PACKAGES

Software packages have been a mixed blessing to business writing. Nowadays you can check spelling, grammar, and readability levels with your computer. However, you can't rely on software exclusively. Documents must still be proofread manually as well as electronically because spell checkers can't catch words that are spelled correctly but are misused, such as *its* versus *it's* and *deer* instead of *dear*.

In addition, grammar packages can indicate errors, and readability indexes can point out the difficulty of the reading level, but for most people the packages don't provide enough information on how to fix the problems they catch. It is up to you to look up any grammar or style points you don't understand — check your grammar book or speak with your English guru. Don't ignore the problem just because you don't understand it. The software package has pointed it out for a reason.

Fortunately, software packages are continually being updated to assist people with their writing. Every upgrade has something extra added. For example, a few years ago you had to purchase a grammar package separately. Now it is a normal feature on word processing programs. The same holds true with spell checkers. Older packages require you to run a separate spell check. Newer packages automatically point out misspelled words as you type them.

Every year, investigate the latest version of your word processing program to see if it has any new features that might make a substantial difference to your writing.

IN SUMMARY

Writing is not static. It constantly changes to match the changes in resources, society, technology, and business. Smart communicators are the ones who recognize that keeping their language skills on the leading edge means success for themselves and their organizations.

The following chapters are designed to provide you with practical guidelines for producing clear, concise letters, memos, reports, faxes, and e-mail messages that meet the needs of today's readers.

2

13 WAYS TO MIND YOUR READER'S BUSINESS AND PUT YOUR OWN ON THE BACK BURNER

One of the main changes in business writing over the past ten years has been in our focus. Even until the late 1970s, senders wrote about what they knew and what they wanted the reader to know. Now effective writers "speak" about what the reader wants to know and needs to know. This change in focus from the sender's interests to the receiver's needs means that writers must understand their readers before they begin to write.

In one of my workshops, a young man firmly opposed this idea. He was "much too busy to consider the reader" before he composed a memo or letter. It was a waste of his time. Yet this same person also admitted his readers didn't always follow through the way he wanted. Nor was it unusual for him to receive phone calls requesting additional information, and sometimes he had to write a second letter to clarify the first. His manager claimed the young man produced dull, lifeless material that often rambled or irritated readers.

Vague ideas, irrelevant details, missing information, inappropriate tone, boring delivery — these are some of the things that can detract from your message if you fail to think about your reader before you write.

There is a marvelous saying that applies both to report and correspondence writing: "Typists pound keyboards and writers stare out windows." In other words, if you busy yourself on your keyboard before you are clear about your reader and the reason for writing, consider yourself a typist. However, if you sit back and think before you begin to type, you will be an effective writer. And if you learn to see through your readers' eyes, talk their language, and present the message in a manner that will appeal to them, then your correspondence will develop an interesting, helpful personality.

Undoubtedly, there are occasions when you don't know much about your reader. If you are answering a letter from a stranger or responding to a quick phone call, you will have to generalize. But the more you focus on your reader, the better your correspondence will be.

Here are some questions to ask yourself about your readers before you begin to write:

1. What is the vocabulary level of your readers? Is English their main language? Are they comfortable with long, complicated words, or are simpler words better? In addition, although long-time residents of a country may know numerous words for an item, new arrivals may know only one.

2. How much education do the readers have? Do they have a general education or are they specialists in the same field as you? Are jargon or "insider" words appropriate?

3. What is the approximate age of the readers? Are they in the workforce? Older readers generally prefer a more formal tone.

   Many baby boomers are reaching the point where they require reading glasses. Ensure that your typeface is a reasonable size.

4. How are you related to the reader? Are you writing to your boss, the public, a client, a potential customer, the president of your company, or the board of directors?

Your tone must change accordingly. Generally, memos to your boss and colleagues are less formal than letters written to clients.

5. What do your readers do for a living? How much understanding do they have of this particular subject? Conveying information of a legal nature to a lawyer requires different words than conveying the same information to a lay person.

6. How many times have you written to these readers about this topic? Is this the first time, so that background details are needed? Is this the second, third, or fourth time you've written? If so, reduce or eliminate the background and concentrate on the current details.

7. What special interests or concerns will the readers have regarding this information? Are you writing a report for politicians whose constituents are affected by your message? If so, you had better include a strong analysis of the pros and cons of your message. Are you writing a proposal to people who believe another company should be the chosen vendor? You will need some strong arguments and some creative thinking to convince them otherwise.

8. Are there any economic or staff constraints that will be foremost in the readers' minds when they read your material? If you are recommending spending money your organization doesn't have, you may be wasting your time with this correspondence, or you may have to be particularly persuasive and explain where the money can be found.

9. What sort of reports do the readers normally want to receive? If you know they prefer reports of no more than two pages in length, don't give them a ten-page document.

If you know they want the recommendation at the top of the first page, that's where you should put it.

10. If your readers are in a different country, their writing rules may differ. It is not only courteous but also good business sense to try to adapt your writing style to theirs.

   The British have a much more formal writing style and tend to use expressions North Americans consider outdated. The British consider the North American "natural" tone disrespectful. Japanese writers are extremely polite and begin letters with references to impersonal topics, such as the weather. Their writing style is indirect, as opposed to the North American desire for clarity and conciseness. In reports, the Japanese tend to present information in chronological order. German reports include detailed background information whether readers require it or not. The tradition in France is to begin reports with the theory behind the problem and follow with the history. Writers from Latin countries often subscribe to the theory "more is best," and include numerous details and adjectives. They tend to play down bad news.

   Stay alert to the different meanings of words. Although English, Spanish, Portuguese, French, and Italian are all based on Latin, they developed differently. Therefore, some words have a different range of meanings according to the country. For example, the French word for a teacher is *le professeur*. However, in English the term *professor* is used only for a teacher at a university.

11. What do the readers need to know about this topic in order to take action? And what do they want to know? As soon as you have focused on this information, you can eliminate all other details.

12. How do you want your readers to react to your message? Do you want them to take some action? In that case, your

request should be concrete, concise, and direct. If the information is bad news, you will want to maintain their goodwill and future cooperation. This affects the organization of the message.

Do you want them to feel some emotion? Do you want them excited about your idea or your product so they'll want it, or do you need them to be concerned so they'll contribute to your charity? This information alters your word choice.

13. Are there any secondary readers? Secondary readers are people to whom a copy of your correspondence is passed. For example, if your boss is pleased with the report you have written, he or she may pass it on to a manager. That manager is your second reader, and the report should be written and organized in a manner that will meet his or her needs.

Worksheet #1 is a planning tool for analyzing your reader. If you use it before you begin to write, you will find that, in the long run, you will produce reports and correspondence more efficiently. In addition, you will start getting the response you want from your readers, as you will be writing more clearly, with the appropriate tone.

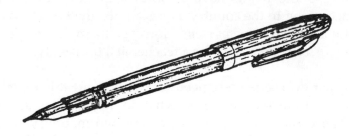

WORKSHEET #1
PLANNING TOOL FOR READER ANALYSIS

PRIMARY READER		
Reader's background		
Relationship to writer		
Vocabulary level	*Basic*	*Standard* *Technical*
Tone	*Informal*	*Semi-formal* *Formal*
Information reader already has		
Details the reader needs to know		
Details the reader wants to know		
Reader's reaction	*Pleased*	*Upset* *Indifferent*
Action you want reader to take		
Are there any secondary readers?		

3

36 PRACTICAL WRITING TIPS YOU NEVER LEARNED IN SCHOOL

Although writing ranks as one of the key skills needed in business today, few people have received extensive training in this area. They have either specialized in courses that require little writing, such as mathematics, or they have taken courses that concentrate on academic writing, which is not the same as business writing.

In the business world, documents are usually written for multiple readers who may not be familiar with the subject matter. Business documents are prepared under time and money constraints. In addition, the readers don't have to — or don't wish to — take the time to sort through and interpret long, complicated messages. Therefore, today's business communications require a style of writing that is concise, clear, and easy to read.

This chapter is devoted to specific, easily adopted tips that ensure your correspondence — whether it travels by "snail mail" or by electronic methods — meets the needs of the marketplace and projects an image of you as a professional, customer-oriented, clear-thinking individual.

THE READER

1. **Knowing your reader is the key to success**. The number one rule of all communications — written or spoken — is to know your audience. Everything hinges on this information. It is so important, I devoted a whole chapter

to it. If you have not yet read chapter 2, I suggest you go back and do so.

WORD CHOICE

2. **Simple words work best.** Reading comprehension studies show that people absorb information faster if it is written slightly below their normal comprehension levels. And if they are in business — whether they are on their own or working for someone else — they don't have time to check a dictionary or ponder the meanings of unfamiliar words.

   Although there are over a million words in the English language, the average adult has a working vocabulary of only 5,000 words and learns just two new words a year. In addition, most of the words in the English language have more than one meaning.

   To ensure that the average reader interprets your message correctly, choose short, simple words. This will reduce the chance for misunderstandings. Table #1 shows a list of words that have been standard fare in business letters and offers you some alternative, simpler words to use in their place.

   Some readers may ask what will happen to the English language if we eliminate the fancy words. But multisyllabic words are still available for creative or recreational writing, which people have more time to read.

3. **Jargon has its place.** Jargon is the technical language used by a specific group or profession. If you're writing for such a group, jargon can explain concepts more clearly and concisely than plain English, and it helps build rapport with a technical

TABLE #1
EASIER-TO-READ WORDS

INSTEAD OF	USE
alleviate	lessen, ease
ameliorate	improve
anticipate	expect
ascertain	determine, find out
as per your request	as you requested
cognizant	aware
consequence	result, outcome
despite the fact that	although
enable	allow, help
endeavor	try
eventuality	result, outcome
expedite	speed up
facilitate	help, aid
forward	send
immediately	now, right away
implement	start
initiate	start, begin
in order to	to
necessitates	requires
notwithstanding	but, despite, regardless
occurrence	event, incident
perusal	review, information
signify	mean
substantiate	support, prove
under no circumstances	never
utilize	use
variation	change
whether or not	if

reader. For example, the word *iterative* is quite common with engineers, but is confusing to most other people. Likewise, *deliverables* is familiar to information systems professionals but leaves others shaking their heads.

Use jargon when you know the word is appropriate for the intended audience. Otherwise, a breakdown in communications could occur.

4. **Each word you write should have a purpose**. Good business writing is economical. Every word is included for a reason: to convey a message, set a tone, or connect ideas. This means all unnecessary words should be eliminated. If two words mean nearly the same thing, the less expressive one should go.

Example	*In addition,* we are *also* sending you our latest brochure.
Better	In addition, we are sending you our latest brochure.
Example	In my past experience (*How many experiences have you had that weren't in your past?*)
Better	In my experience
Example	First and foremost
Better	First

The word *that* is often overused. Whenever you find yourself writing it, read the sentence aloud to determine if you really need it. Most of the time, the sentence reads better without it.

Example	I understand *that* you are looking for a new account manager.
Better	I understand you need a new account manager.

5. **Intensive words, such as** *very, highly, greatly,* **and** *extremely,* **detract from your professional image.** Intensives should be used with care. They lean toward overstatement, which may cause the reader to doubt your reliability. They also imply information that cannot be measured, as everyone gives the words his or her own subjective meaning.

Example	I was *very* pleased to talk with you last week regarding…
Better	I was pleased to talk with you last week regarding…

6. **Connecting words or phrases will help you "drive" your reader through your material.** Words such as *however, in addition,* and *to summarize* signal the reader that the upcoming statement supports (green light), conflicts with (red light), or illustrates (yellow light) the preceding point. Table #2 lists some connecting words you can use to move your writing along in different situations.

   If you don't use connecting words, your writing will appear disjointed. Readers will be forced to interpret it themselves; they may even give up and turn to easier-to-read material.

   Note: Sentences may begin with *and* or *but*. Although this practice was frowned upon years ago, these words serve as excellent connectors in memos and informal letters — they make it sound as if we are talking to our reader — and it is now acceptable to use them.

7. **Clichés are boring.** Clichés are words and phrases that were refreshing in bygone years. Now they are meaningless. You might get away with the occasional cliché, but too many will give your correspondence a stilted, insincere tone. Table #3 lists common clichés and their modern replacements.

TABLE #2
CONNECTING WORDS AND PHRASES

PURPOSE	FORMAL	INFORMAL
Comparison	similarly, in comparison	again, likewise, still
Time	eventually, formerly, subsequently	then, next, after, later, since, while
Same direction	furthermore, moreover, in addition	and, first, second, third, besides, also
Contrast	however, nevertheless, on the contrary	but, still, yet, meanwhile, on the other hand
Illustration	to illustrate, in other words	for example
Conclusion	therefore, accordingly, in conclusion	so, as a result, to sum up, in short
Emphasis	in any event, to be sure	of course, naturally, obviously

8. **Strong verbs create powerful messages**. Many writers unconsciously take strong verbs and turn them into nouns. Then they search for another verb to fit the sentence. Not only does this rob sentences of their strength and vitality, but it adds additional, unnecessary words.

   To remedy this problem, go over your writing and "flag" all words ending with *-ance, -ment,* and *-tion.* Whenever possible, replace these words with a verb.

TABLE #3
CLICHÉS TO AVOID

CLICHÉ	UPDATE
At your earliest convenience At an early date, Recent date, At this time	*If you have a date, give it.*
At this writing, At this point in time	*If you mean now,* *say "now."*
Attached please find Please find enclosed Enclosed please find You will find	Attached is/are Enclosed is/are Enclosed is/are Here is/are
Hereto/herewith/hereby/ said/above/same/thereof/ wherein/hereinafter	*These words are legalese.* *Delete them.*
I remain	*Old-fashioned — delete*
Permit me to say	*Useless filler — delete*
I would like to take this opportunity to	*Useless filler — delete*
This letter is for the purpose of	*Useless filler — delete*
We wish to acknowledge receipt of	We have received
As per your request, Pursuant to your request, Referring to your request, In reference to your letter	As requested, As you requested in your letter of May 3
The writer, The undersigned	Me, I
Thanking you in advance	Thank you for…
Under separate cover	Separately

Example	This letter *is a confirmation* of the details of our meeting last Tuesday.
Better	This letter *confirms* the details of last Tuesday's meeting.
Example	*Preparation* of an agenda should be done before a meeting.
Better	*Prepare* an agenda before the meeting.

9. **Helping verbs aren't always helpful**. There is a category of verbs called helping verbs. They help other verbs express their meanings. However, they can weaken a message. Whenever possible, replace them with strong action verbs.

Helping verbs include:

- Be (am, is, are, was, were, been)
- Have (has, had)
- Do (does, did)
- Shall
- Should
- Would

Example	I *will have* (helping verbs) completed the project by Friday.
Better	I will complete the project by Friday.
Example	I *have been* (helping verbs) invited to tour the plant.
Better	I am invited to tour the plant.

Note: Eliminating all helping verbs is impossible. But every time you delete or replace one, your sentence becomes stronger.

10. **Verbs and phrases should inspire confidence**. *Would, might,* and *could* are weak verbs. Delete them, or replace them with the more positive words *will* and *can*.

Example   Would you please send us a copy of the financial statement?

Better   Will you please send us a copy of the financial statement?

Better   Please send us a copy of the financial statement.

11. **Impersonal phrases weaken ideas**. Impersonal phrases such as *it was suggested, it seems, it appears, we should consider, we seem to be in favor,* and *it may be that...* are too tentative. Whenever you use these wimpy phrases, you lose credibility. Eliminate them.

Example   It appears the figures are inaccurate.

Better   The figures are inaccurate.

12. **Be careful when using abbreviations**. Abbreviations are shortened forms of words. They may consist of the first few letters, such as *Nov.* for *November,* or just the consonants, *amt.* for *amount.* These types of abbreviations make a writer appear lazy. Take the time to write the words in full, and give yourself the image of an energetic professional. Avoid *etc.*

Example   At our next meeting, we will discuss forecasting, customer surveys, new leads, etc.

Better   At our next meeting, some of the items we will discuss are forecasting, customer surveys, and new leads.

Better   At our next meeting, some of the items we will discuss are the following:
        • forecasting,

- customer surveys, and
- new leads.

Other abbreviations are formed from the initial letters of words. For example, *Credit Valley Hospital* becomes *CVH*. Too many abbreviations of this type make readers feel they are looking at a bowl of alphabet soup. If you do need the occasional abbreviation for faster reading, make sure you define it the first time you use it.

Example   Credit Valley Hospital (CVH) is known for its commitment to community involvement. Staff from CVH regularly volunteer at the food bank.

Note: If more than five pages have passed since you spelled out an acronym or abbreviation, the reader may have forgotten what it stands for. You should redefine it.

SENTENCES

13. **The first and last words of a sentence stand out**. People read the same way they watch a situation comedy on TV. They turn on in the beginning, tune out in the middle, come back for the end, and assume they understand what went on. Be careful you don't bury crucial information in the middle of a long sentence. It may get overlooked.

Example   In the near future, sales will be hiring two new account managers as we work on improving our customer service. (*In the near future* stands out, as does *improving our customer service*.)

Better   Two new account managers, who will be hired by sales in the near future, will help us improve customer service. (*Two new account managers* and *improve customer service* are now the key points.)

14. **The average length of a sentence in business writing is 15 words**. This is the easiest length for a reader to absorb quickly.

15. **Sentences with more than 40 words irritate readers**. Sentences over 40 words tend to frustrate readers. They will either skip over details or interpret the message incorrectly. Break long sentences into two or three shorter ones.

    Example Our intent in forwarding the list of priority short-term capital projects in advance of the final report has been to fast track the approval process in anticipation of a review of each capital project to be conducted by government staff with your staff.

    Better Attached is the list of priority short-term capital projects. We are sending you this information before the final report is released in an effort to fast track the approval process. This early release of the information should give your staff an opportunity to be prepared when the anticipated government review takes place.

16. **The best correspondence includes a variety of sentence lengths**. Too many long sentences are confusing. Too many short sentences read like baby talk. A variety of lengths appeals to readers.

17. **Sentences requiring more than four pieces of punctuation are hard to read**. A sentence that includes so many details it requires this much punctuation will be difficult for your reader to digest. Break it into two or more sentences. (Don't forget to count the period or question mark at the end of the sentence.)

    Example In addition, I would recommend the board make a priority of a five-year planning document, which is scheduled to be presented, as part of its annual review process, to senior management in the first week of March.

Better In addition, I recommend the department make the preparation of a five-year planning document a priority. The document is scheduled for presentation to senior management in March as part of the annual review process.

Note: This technique will also help you present your points in a logical, easy-to-read manner.

18. **Lists are the best way to convey three or more points**. Point-form lists help the reader absorb information, and they provide white space (see Rule #26).

Example There are three possible solutions under the present legislation: use only the locations accessible to the handicapped, renovate poorly designed locations, or install temporary ramps.

Better There are three possible solutions under the present legislation:

- Use only the locations accessible to the handicapped.
- Renovate poorly designed locations.
- Install temporary ramps.

Note: Use punctuation with lists if the points are expressed in complete sentences or long phrases (as in the example above). No periods are required if the sentences are short (see the list at Rule #12); otherwise, use no punctuation — even after the final item. Capitalizing the first letter of each point is optional, but be consistent with your choice. If the phrases are essential to the grammatical correctness of the statement introducing the list (e.g., see the list on page xiv), then use the appropriate punctuation.

You can use numbers, letters, or dashes (—) instead of bullets (•); however, numbers and letters may give your readers the impression that the first point deserves more attention than the last. If points are listed in order of importance, use numbers.

Don't forget to indent your lists so they stand out on the page.

19. **Good news should be placed in a short sentence, preferably in a short paragraph.** Good news stands out more clearly if it is in a short, easy-to-read sentence.

   Example   This year, after a careful fine-tuning of our budget, we were able to reduce our administrative costs by a grand total of $300,000.

   Better   This year we saved $300,000 in administrative costs.

20. **Bad news should never be delivered in a short sentence, unless you are deliberately trying to upset a reader.** Soften bad news by putting it in a longer sentence and defusing the message.

   Example   The report will be a week late.

   Better   The report will be a week late, but it will include the latest figures.

   Example   The repairs will cost $12,000.

   Better   Although the repairs will cost $12,000, additional work will not be required for two years.

21. **Active voice sentences are preferable, but don't throw out all passive voice sentences.** Voice is a grammatical term that refers to the relationship between a subject and verb in a sentence. In the active voice, the person or thing that is the subject is doing the acting and appears at the beginning of the sentence. In the passive voice, often

called backward writing, the subject is being acted upon, and often appears at the end of the sentence, or is missing.

Examples Suzanne Watson handled the customer's complaint. *(active voice)*

The customer's complaint was handled by Suzanne Watson. *(passive voice)*

Use Form 2-11 to record any variations in standard procedures. *(active voice — the "you" is understood)*

Any variations in standard procedures should be recorded on Form 2-11. *(passive voice)*

Accomplished letter and memo writers make a conscious decision when to use the passive voice because it:

(a) uses more words

(b) is not as direct as the active voice

(c) gives your writing a more formal tone

On the other hand, don't eliminate the passive voice entirely. It is ideal for presenting negative findings in a report or for pointing out a problem when you don't want to place specific blame. Technical reports and formal minutes are often written in the passive voice because the *what* is more important than the *who*.

Example You should not make critical remarks in public. *(active voice)*

Example Critical remarks should not be made in public. *(passive voice)*

PARAGRAPHS

22. **Opening and closing paragraphs in letters, memos, and reports should not be more than four to six lines long.** Business writing is psychological. If your opening

paragraphs are too long, they will discourage your readers from taking the time to continue reading. Sample #1 shows a letter with a long opening paragraph. In Sample #2, this paragraph has been broken into three parts. The opening paragraph is shorter, and the sub-head provides more white space.

Closing paragraphs should also be brief, and they should clearly indicate the action the reader is to take. If this information is conveyed clearly and concisely, you are more likely to get the results you want.

23. **Paragraphs in the body of a letter, memo, or report should never exceed ten lines**. Again, today's readers are intimidated by long chunks of information. They will read the first and last sentences and skim the middle. Therefore, to ensure that your reader will not miss important information, keep paragraphs under ten lines long. Sample #1 shows a letter with long paragraphs; Sample #2 shows how the same text can be made more appealing and easier to read.

24. **Opening and closing paragraphs for e-mail should be two to three lines long; body paragraphs should never exceed five lines**. Reading from a computer screen is more difficult than reading hard copy. If your e-mail paragraph fills the screen, your reader may not try to interpret it. Make it easy on your reader — keep your paragraphs short.

APPEARANCE

25. **Appearance is important**. Most people don't plan the appearance of their documents. Yet how a letter, memo, or report looks plays a major role in whether or not the receiver reads it. If it appears too difficult to read, the receiver may ignore the material or put off reading it to a more convenient time.

Dear Mr. Belmont:

As you are no doubt aware, personal computers play a paramount role in industry today. As these sophisticated systems take over more and more business functions, our dependence on them is growing dramatically. However, computers and peripheral equipment do break down. In fact, industry research indicates that the typical microcomputer system will need servicing at least twice a year. When it does, you are faced with downtime, reduced productivity, and often a large repair bill. The Echo Maintenance Agreement Program has been designed to combat the worries that often accompany extensive microcomputer usage, no matter how small or large your system may be.

Echo is qualified to service microcomputer and peripheral equipment for more than 40 manufacturers, including hundreds of product configurations. No matter what system your company has invested in, chances are that Echo can service it. Echo has been authorized by many manufacturers to provide full warranty service, thereby ending the delays in shipping your micro or peripheral equipment to a factory for repairs. In addition, we have set up nationwide service centers to provide you with a convenient, local service. Each center has an independent parts inventory as well as a link-up to our international inventory system.

You have the choice of pick-up delivery, carry-in, or on-site servicing — whatever is the most convenient and cost effective for you and your company's requirements.

...2

Dear Mr. Belmont:

As you are no doubt aware, personal computers play a paramount role in industry today. As these sophisticated systems take over more and more business functions, our dependence on them is growing dramatically.

Computers and peripheral equipment, however, do break down. In fact, industry research indicates that the typical microcomputer system will need servicing at least twice a year. When it does, you are faced with downtime, reduced productivity, and often a large repair bill. The Echo Maintenance Agreement Program has been designed to combat the worries that often accompany extensive microcomputer usage, no matter how small or large your system may be.

Echo is qualified to service microcomputer and peripheral equipment for more than 40 manufacturers, including hundreds of product configurations. No matter what system your company has invested in, chances are that Echo can service it. Echo has been authorized by many manufacturers to provide full warranty service, thereby ending the delays in shipping your micro or peripheral equipment to a factory for repairs.

Warranty Service
We have set up nationwide service centers to provide you with a convenient, local service. Each center has an independent parts inventory as well as a link-up to our international inventory system.

You have the choice of pick-up delivery, carry-in, or on-site servicing — whatever is the most convenient.

...2

26. **White space is crucial**. White space is any space left unprinted. It includes the margins and the space between paragraphs and around lists. White space gives your readers' eyes a micro-second chance to rest and a micro-second chance to absorb the message. Documents with an attractive balance between white space and print appeal to readers. Although determining the correct balance is subjective, if you keep your paragraphs short, use lists, and use subheads, you will have an attractive, easy-to-read page.

27. **Margins are a key part of appearance**. All written documents should have margins at least one inch wide on all four sides. The margins will increase depending on the dictates of the letterhead and whether the document is bound.

    Letters should be centered between the top and bottom of the page; memos begin at the top of the page.

28. **Typefaces should be easy to read**. With today's word processors, you have access to numerous fonts. However, if you **use too many different ones**, YOU'LL END UP with a "ransom note" effect.

    Use only one *serif* (a typeface with short lines projecting from the strokes in each letter) and one sans serif (a typeface with no extra lines on the letters) typeface per document. Text is generally easier to read in a serif typeface; overheads, slides, and computer screens are better in a sans serif typeface. Some serif fonts are Baskerville, Bookman, and Times Roman. Common sans serif fonts are Helvetica, Univers, and Avant Garde.

    A fairly common practice for reports is to use Times Roman or Bookman for the body and Helvetica for the headings and sub-headings. You can vary the look by using different sizes of the two fonts; for example, use 18-point Helvetica for a heading and the same font at 14 points for a sub-head. For a more complex report, you could use Univers for the headlines, Helvetica for the sub-heads, and Baskerville for the text. As a rule of thumb, do not use more than three different fonts per document.

29. **Choose your font size carefully**. Don't choose a smaller font in an attempt to get all the information on one page. If your font size is so small and your margins so narrow that more than 90 characters fit on a line, your reader will have trouble reading the material. (When counting characters, include spaces and punctuation.)

Likewise, your reader will find it difficult if you can fit only 30 characters on a line. This size of font causes rapid back-and-forth eye movement that is irritating.

The size of font you choose depends on your typeface. If you are using Bookman, I suggest 12 point. Another common font and type size is 12-point Times Roman. However, if the message if lengthy, some people find this hard on the eyes. My personal preference is 14-point Times Roman.

Before you decide on a particular font and type size, print out a few paragraphs in a variety of styles so you can choose the most readable one for your audience.

30. **Increase leading if type is small**. If your line contains more than 60 characters, add space between the lines to make the words easier to read. A good guideline is to set the line space — or leading (rhymes with "heading") — two points greater than the point size of the font.

If you don't know how to increase the leading, ask your resident computer guru. It is a quick, simple step.

31. **Be careful when deciding whether to justify the type on your page**. Justification is the term given to how text is arranged on the page. If every line begins at the left

margin and ends exactly at the right margin, the page is said to be justified. A nonjustified or, as it is sometimes called, a ragged right style is one where the lines end near, but not always exactly at, the right margin.

If you don't have proportional spacing on your word processor, don't justify; it will cause odd-looking spaces. Most people find text with a ragged right margin easier to read because of the even word spacing, logical word breaks, and additional white space.

32. **Never type the entire body of any document or e-mail in capital letters, italics, or boldface**. Believing that it adds style or interest, some people use italics, boldface, or capitals for large portions of, or for the entire text of, a document. However, these typefaces are hard to read, and when they are overused they are not available for their usual function — to add special emphasis to a word or phrase.

Never use italics for an entire business letter as they project an overly casual appearance.

Note: One of the most common complaints about e-mail is that senders often use all capital letters, making the message difficult to read.

33. **Use capital letters, bolding, and italics for emphasis only**. Use italics for emphasis, all capitals for more emphasis, and bolding to hold and catch the reader's eye. Don't get carried away. Don't underline the same information that you have already bolded. This is wasting a valuable tool. In addition, too much bolding or underlining distracts the reader from your message.

Examples We can register you *if you fill in the attached documents.*

FILL IN THE ATTACHED DOCUMENTS and we will register you.

To be registered, **you must fill in the attached documents**.

Wrong   To be registered, <u>**you must fill in the attached documents.**</u> *(overkill)*

Italics or underlining can be used for references to complete published works such as books, pamphlets, magazines, newspapers, and legislation.

Examples Enclosed is a copy of our brochure *Holding a Successful Workshop*.

Please note the article "Public Speaking for Shrinking Violets" in this month's *Successful Business* magazine.

34. **Sub-heads are ideal for breaking up long chunks of text**. Sub-heads appeal to readers. They make it easier to understand and interpret the message; they also make the writer look organized.

In long letters, try to use at least one sub-head per page — whenever you are making a new point. In reports, aim for a sub-head every five or six paragraphs.

35. **Make your sub-heads as descriptive as possible**. The best sub-head is one that adequately describes the upcoming information, so if readers only skim the material they will still have a basic understanding of your message. Sub-heads can run as long as seven or eight words.

Example Warranty Package

Better   New Warranty Package for Large-Screen TVs

Once you have written a letter, report, or other document, go over it with Checklist #1 and make sure your writing and presentation are as strong and clear as possible.

CHECKLIST #1
BUSINESS WRITING STYLE

After you have written your document, ask yourself these questions:

WORD CHOICE

☐ Will my reader immediately understand each word?

☐ Did I use jargon, abbreviations, or acronyms?
Were they appropriate and understandable?

☐ Did I use connecting words to move my reader through
the message?

☐ Did I avoid clichés?

☐ Can I replace any of the helping verbs or nouns ending
in *-ance, -ment,* and *-tion*?

☐ Did I eliminate any weak verbs or phrases?

SENTENCES

☐ Are all my sentences less than 40 words?

☐ Did I use a variety of sentence lengths?
Is the average length approximately 15 words?

☐ Did I write any sentence that required more than four
pieces of punctuation?

☐ Are most of my sentences in the active voice?

☐ Were negative findings reported in passive voice
sentences?

☐ Did I use lists to introduce a series of ideas?

☐ Is good news in short sentences, bad news in longer
sentences?

PARAGRAPHS

☐ Are all my paragraphs less than ten lines long in written
correspondence and less than five lines in an e-mail?

☐ Are opening and closing paragraphs less than four to
six lines? Two to three lines for e-mail?

APPEARANCE

☐ Is the size and font of the typeface easy to read?

☐ Does the text look balanced on the page?

☐ Is there plenty of white space?

☐ Did I bold and underline appropriate words only?

☐ Did I break up large chunks of copy with sub-heads?

---

36. **The tone of your communications can win you friends or earn you enemies.** Tone is the way you express yourself in your communications with others. You can come across as boring, enthusiastic, caring, or overly formal. Tone is so important that chapter 4 deals entirely with this topic. Read on.

4

26 WAYS TO ADD PERSONALITY TO YOUR WRITING AND WIN FRIENDS

In addition to clarity and conciseness, effective business correspondence must have a good tone.

Tone is the way a message sounds. It adds personality to your writing. It turns messages into interesting and refreshing correspondence, or it reduces them to bland and boring documents. It can create goodwill and strengthen business relationships, or it can confuse and finally irritate readers. A poor tone makes a message — even an exciting one — uninteresting.

Example It is with our deepest and sincere good wishes that we hereby wish to acknowledge receipt of the news that you have been appointed vice-president of your company.

Better Congratulations. We hear you are the new vice-president of Dohickeroo.

If you had to choose one of the following two writers to do business with, which one would you contact first?

Poor tone I would like to take this opportunity to thank you for visiting our booth at the COMTACTS show last week.

Enclosed are the brochures you requested.

If I can be of further assistance, please do not hesitate to contact me.

Sincerely,

Improved tone
I enjoyed talking with you at the COMTACTS show last week and discussing your plans for upgrading your system.

Enclosed are the brochures you requested. I believe the one entitled *Computers and People: A necessary alliance* will answer many of your concerns regarding compatibility.

I will phone you next week after you have had a chance to go over the material. If you have any more questions, I'll be glad to answer them. If I can't, I'll put you in touch with our resident expert.

Cordially,

Only one or two generations ago, it was the style for writers to produce letters and reports that all sounded alike. Anyone who refused to apply the established phrases and formats was considered eccentric or radical.

Now, especially in our letters, readers want to see some personality. They want to know who they are doing business with. They want to feel a rapport between you and them, between your company and their company. Your tone is what does this for you. It involves sentence length and voice, word choice and contractions, and the way you address the reader. Tone can make you and your organization seem cold, unbending, and mechanical or pleasant, friendly, and caring.

Readers want to see some personality.

DIFFERENT KINDS OF TONE

Following are four different ways to write the same message.

Cold   Please find enclosed documents regarding the widget project for your perusal. Your verbal analysis is required at the meeting scheduled for next Monday.

Formal   A report on the widget project is attached for your review. We would appreciate hearing your observations at next Monday's meeting.

Semi-formal   Please review the attached widget report. We look forward to hearing your comments at next Monday's meeting.

Informal   Here is the widget report. Let us know what you think at Monday's meeting.

Notice that I haven't labeled these statements good, better, or best. Each statement (except for the one marked "Cold") is acceptable at different times. The tone must change according to the occasion (see Table #4). For example, if you are writing upward, that is, writing to people who are above you in the office hierarchy, you should adopt a semi-formal tone rather than an informal one.

TABLE #4
TONE

FORMAL	SEMI-FORMAL	INFORMAL
Annual reports	Letters	Letters (*to long-time associates*)
Technical reports	Memos, Reports	Memos
Formal minutes	Writing upward	E-mail

Normally, reports are written in a formal, impersonal tone. There are two reasons for this. First, there are usually several readers and the writer may not be familiar with each person. Second, good reports contain facts, statistics, and technical information. There is no room for the writer's personality and subjective viewpoint. Occasionally a report may be written in a less formal style, but this occurs only when the report is for in-house use and is going to a small, selected audience. This kind of report is usually written as a memo.

How do you write in a formal tone?

- Write all words in full. Don't use contractions such as *it's*, *can't*, and *don't* (replace them with *it is, cannot*, and *do not*).

- Refer to people by title or job description if necessary, not by their names.

- Avoid the words *I* or *me*, although a faceless *we* may be appropriate.

- Use passive verbs, particularly when presenting negative findings.

- Use longer sentences and paragraphs (but none over ten lines long).

Letters, memos, and e-mails are different. There is no reason they have to be dry and colorless. In fact, the majority should read as if a warm-blooded, live person wrote them.

Too many people believe they have to "change hats" when they write. And the hats they put on are heavy, unbecoming, and old-fashioned. These writers haven't stopped to realize what they are doing. They learned to write from their teachers and parents who in turn learned to write from their teachers and parents. Each generation carried on the language and tone of people and businesses no longer in existence.

This is illogical for today's business world, where people like things that are different. Now the most successful business letters possess a person-to-person, friendly air.

If you are uncertain how personable your correspondence sounds to others, read some of your letters and memos aloud. Ask yourself:

- Does this sound like me?

- Are these the words I would use on the phone or when talking to someone?

- If I were the reader, how would I feel? Would I wish to do business with this person?

Some people have a natural gift for putting themselves into their message. However, if you are not happy with the tone of your letters, or feel there is room for improvement, here are some tips that are sure to help.

STARTING TO WRITE

1. **Begin by thinking about the reader and your purpose in writing**. Look at your message from the other person's viewpoint. Choose words you think the reader prefers, and arrange them in ways he or she won't resent.

2. **Relax when you write**. The best letters flow from the heart. They are simple, natural and get to the point.

   Approach the task not as "I have to write to her" but as "I am going to talk to her." Do not take this too literally; don't use slang or ignore the rules of grammar. Just write in a respectful, friendly way — the same way you would talk to educated friends.

3. **Watch the opening words of your correspondence**. If you want to jump-start your letters, be careful with the first few words of your opening. Unnecessary fillers create a cold tone that is hard to warm up.

Example   I wish to take this opportunity to thank you for talking to me on the phone last week about job opportunities with your firm.

Better   Thank you for talking with me on the phone last week regarding job opportunities.

4. **Opening lines improve when you start with people rather than things**.

Example   Enclosed please find the brochure you requested.

Better   As you requested, here is the brochure.

5. **Don't start with a mention of office procedures**. Opening with words such as *according to our files* or *our records indicate* kills the reader's enthusiasm immediately. It gives people the impression you thought about them only when you were reminded to do so by your files.

Example   According to our files, you weren't happy with your latest shipment.

Better   I understand there were some difficulties associated with your latest shipment.

BEING COURTEOUS

6. **Use *I* more than *we***. *We* means the organization and *I* means you personally. You can use both words in your correspondence. However, when it is practical and more accurate, use *I* over *we*. It adds personality to your writing and shows you are willing to take responsibility.

Example   If we can be of further assistance, please call us.

Better   If I can be of further assistance, please call me at 555-4567.

7. **Use *you* more than *I* or *me***. Everyone listens to radio station WIIFM (What's in it for me). You'll obtain a

greater response from your readers when you spend more time talking to them than blowing your own horn.

Example   I am available at your convenience to discuss this issue further.

Better   If you wish to discuss this issue further, please let me know.

8. **Use personal words**. A good method for determining how appealing your message is to the reader is to count the number of personal references. Personal references are words such as *I, me, you, he, she, it, we, they, your,* and *mine,* and names of people and companies. A rough guideline is that there should be six personal words for every 100 words.

Example   If the most recent business writing trends were tracked, *it* would be evident that an increased number of faxes and e-mails are being sent out to clients, customers, and staff. And the number of formal business letters is most likely down from a few years ago, when everyone had a secretary to type them, check them for spelling and punctuation, and arrange the layout on the page. (67 words, 1 personal reference.)

Better   If *you* were to track the most recent business writing trends, *you* would find an increased number of faxes and e-mails are being sent out to *your* clients, customers, and staff. The number of formal business letters *you* write is most likely down from a few years ago, when *you* had a secretary to type them, check them for spelling and punctuation, and arrange the layout on the page. (68 words, 5 personal references.)

9. **Use the reader's name**. A person's proudest possession is his or her name. Use it. When you are speaking, people

can't tell if you are using the proper spelling, but they know in a letter. So check and double-check it.

Use the name at least once in a one- to one-and-a-half-page letter, but don't tie it in with negative thoughts.

Example   I have not yet received your expense account, Jeff.

Better   Jeff, if you send me your expense account tomorrow, I can cut you a check before the weekend.

If the salutation line begins formally with *Dear Mr. Jones:*, stick with that name in the body of your letter. If it begins *Dear Greg,* use the first name in the body.

To decide whether to call people by their first or last names, think about how you would address them if you were meeting them in their office. Remember, though, if you start with *Dear Suzanne,* you shouldn't switch back to *Dear Ms. Watson:* in future letters. It gives the impression you no longer wish to be friendly.

Note: If this is your first communication with a reader who is not part of your organization, don't use his or her first name. Many readers are irritated when someone they have never met becomes too friendly too fast.

10. **Avoid condescending words**. If you use words and phrases such as *obviously, it is clear,* and *as you are aware,* you may appear patronizing and could antagonize your reader.

    Example   Obviously, you are unaware of our refund policy.

    Better   Our refund policy covers...

11. **Be polite**. When you ask someone to do something, it's common courtesy to add the words *please, thank you,* or *I*

would appreciate. (Incidentally, the word *kindly* is old-fashioned and should not be used in business. Replace it with *please.*)

Example   Please call me next week with the details.

I'd appreciate a call next week regarding the details.

But make sure the words of courtesy fit. For example, don't start every letter with *thank you* or you'll sound insincere, particularly when you are responding to a letter of complaint.

Example   Thank you for your letter of May 16 in which you complained about our service program.

Better   After receiving your letter of May 16, I reviewed your concerns with our service department.

You can also use *thank you* to close your letter, if you haven't previously written it in the opening lines or body. The phrase *thank you, again* smacks of insincerity or boredom.

12. **Smooth over awkward refusals with kind words.** Use conditional words such as *could, would, might, wish,* and *if* to soften refusals.

Example   I cannot attend the strategic planning retreat.

Better   I would attend the strategic planning retreat, but then I would miss my son's graduation.

Example   I can't accept your invitation.

Better   I wish I could accept your invitation.

13. **The more contractions you use, the more conversational your writing will sound.** *Don't, can't, won't,* and other contractions should be avoided in reports, but they work well when you want to adopt a less formal tone.

Formal	The committee has not yet reached a decision.
Semi-formal	The committee hasn't reached a decision yet.
Informal	The committee hasn't decided yet.

SELLING YOUR MESSAGE

14. **Accentuate the positive**. Tell readers what you can do — not what you can't.

Example	We cannot begin shipping until September 2.
Better	We will begin shipping on September 2.

15. **Use short, informal sentences**. Incorporating shorter sentences gives you a more conversational tone.

Example	I want to thank you for your consideration in telephoning me about your recent confusion over the policy.
Better	Thank you for telephoning me about the policy.

16. **Turn a demand into a question, or use a cause-and-effect approach**. Instead of demanding readers do something immediately, soften your approach by phrasing the request as a question, or by telling them what you will do if they complete the task.

Example	You must sign this form and return it to us by February 15 or your name will not be added to the list of people who require snow shoveling.
Better	Will you please sign and return this form by February 15? That way we can add your name to the list of people who require snow shoveling. *(Question approach)*
Better	As soon as we receive the signed form, we will add your name to the list of people requiring snow shoveling. *(Cause-and-effect approach)*

17. **Use active voice rather than passive**. The active voice indicates you are taking responsibility for what is happening and reveals you as an individual.

Example   Your letter was received by us on May 2.

Better   I received your letter on May 2.

18. **Add a personal touch**. If you are writing to someone you know well, develop a personal touch. How can you do this? Include an extra line about that person, the city he or she lives in, a previous contact, or anything that may be of mutual interest. Usually "extras" are typed near the end of a letter, or written in ink when the writer signs it.

Example   I heard you were vacationing in Jamaica last week. I look forward to hearing your comments on that interesting island.

19. **Always explain benefits to your readers**. Too many writers, when listing features of a product or service, don't explain what benefit the reader will receive, leaving it up to the readers to work this out for themselves. When you are selling your readers on an idea, product, or service, spell out the advantages to them. Not only does this technique have a better audience response, but it also makes you appear more interested in, and knowledgeable about, your readers' needs.

Example   We have a 24-hour hot line service.

Better   Our 24-hour hot line guarantees you will never have to wait more than a few minutes for the answers to any of your questions.

20. **Put "sell" into everything you write**. Whenever you write, do something to stimulate goodwill. Even if you are just answering a simple request, remember the people who requested the information may spend money with your organization in the future. Is there anything you can

45

write to confirm their judgment that they are dealing with a professional, caring person who works for an organization dedicated to its products and customer service? One extra sentence is sometimes all it takes to turn a routine reply into a positive selling tool.

Example   Here is the brochure you requested at the computer show.

Better   Here is the brochure you requested at the computer show. I have highlighted the paragraphs dealing with your specific software applications.

Example   Thank you for your interest in *Straight Talk*. The cost for 250 copies is 30¢ each. It would be a pleasure to serve you.

Better   Thank you for your interest in *Straight Talk*. We believe it is the best newsletter on business writing today. A number of companies use it to ensure their staff keep up to date with grammar rules and changes in writing styles. The cost for 250 copies is $75. As soon as we receive your check or purchase order, we'll send your order by courier.

21. **Push, don't pull, your readers**. Your readers will respond better if you try to interest them in doing what you want, rather than demanding they do it.

Example   Failure to provide us with your check by August 1 will mean a cancellation of your registration.

Better   If we do not receive your check by August 1, we will have to cancel your registration.

Better   If you send us your check by August 1, we will renew your registration.

46

22. **Send out brief congratulatory or thank-you notes**. One good way to keep your name in front of your customers and clients is to send out short notes congratulating them or thanking them for some activity. Yes, you could phone them, but chances are you'll end up on their voice mail. Besides, written statements produce a visual impact that remains longer in the memory. They can also be filed or shown to superiors and colleagues.

Take care, however, that these notes don't become routine. Each one should be a personalized message to the reader. When notes read as if they are prepared by someone else and barely glanced at by the person who signed them, they lose their value.

I recently met a real estate agent who told me she sends out eight thank-you cards a day. "Eight!" I exclaimed. It seemed like a lot. "Yes," she replied. "That's all I need in order to earn $25,000 a year." (And real estate is not the easiest market to be in nowadays.) If she couldn't think of eight people to write to, she would go out and deliberately look for people and things she could praise.

23. **Be careful with humor. It may get you into trouble**. Humor is always good to relieve tension and get a point across in a lighter vein. However, people understand humor not only through the words but also through body language and voice inflection. In letters, memos, and reports, readers do not have access to these clues and comments may be badly misinterpreted.

The membership chair of a large group once sent out the following statement: *I would personally appreciate your sending in your check because I have other things I would rather spend my limited time doing than following up with your renewal.* The chair claimed it was written with tongue in cheek, but no one was amused. In fact, many members were irritated. How would you react?

In e-mails, many people use "smileys:" symbols that replace body language. (For more information on smileys see chapter 8.)

24. **Never write when you are cross or irritable**. If you are annoyed, it will show up in your writing. No matter how you phrase the words, the tone will be abrupt and the reader will sense the upset. It is better to delay the writing to another time, or write the letter and give it at least a day's simmering period before you revise and mail it out.

Never write when you are cross or irritable.

Example   Please provide us with a memo outlining your specific requirements in terms of documentation from a builder in this situation so that we will no longer provide builders with an inconsistent message when we are advising them on the paperwork they must complete. *(The writer who penned these words was obviously ticked off.)*

Better   To ensure builders receive a consistent message on how to deal with this situation, please send us a memo stating the documents you require.

25. **Don't go overboard**. A pleasant, friendly tone is important, but don't overdo it, especially if you don't know the reader or if you know the reader prefers a more formal

form of speech. And don't gush. It only makes you seem insincere.

Example   In spending so much time answering my questions last week, you rose even higher in my estimation and consolidated the fact that you are truly among the great individuals in life, dedicated to excellence and committed to assisting others in achieving their goals.

Better   I appreciate the time you took in answering my questions last week. I can see why so many people hold you in such high regard.

26. **Read your letters aloud**. Read your letter out loud and listen to it. Does it have a natural, friendly flow or is it choppy and demanding? If you were the reader, would you like the writer?

    Your tone should be part of your overall business strategy. It is an expression of the business relationship you wish to foster with the reader. Initially, the tone should be semi-formal, moving slowly toward the informal side as the business relationship and friendship develop. Be careful not to edge over to the informal too quickly, as it is hard to return to the formal relationship once you've gotten close.

    Finally, when you have decided on the tone you wish to adopt, use it consistently throughout the entire letter. If you are writing to a dignitary, start with a formal tone and stay with it, even to the complimentary closing. If you begin with a conversational tone, don't become cold and impersonal halfway through. Always be consistent.

    To make sure you maintain a consistent tone, evaluate your writing using Checklist #2.

CHECKLIST #2
APPROPRIATE TONE

After you have written your first draft, ask yourself:

☐ Did I think about the reader before I started the document?

☐ Did I deliberately choose a tone that reflects my relationship to the reader?

☐ Do the words sound natural and not stuffy?

☐ Do my opening words get quickly into the message and avoid boring the reader?

☐ Did I use more you words than I words?

☐ If I listed the features of any idea, service, or product, did I also include the benefits to the reader?

☐ Did I try to soften negative news?

☐ Is my tone consistent throughout the entire document?

☐ If I were the reader, would I like to do business with the writer of this document?

5

42 WAYS TO MASTER LETTERS AND MAKE YOURSELF LOOK PROFESSIONAL ON PAPER

There are no unimportant letters. Each one is an opportunity to win friends, influence people, build better customer relations, and keep your name in front of existing or potential clients.

Letters can be sent to confirm or request information, deal with misunderstandings and complaints, sell new ideas and services, congratulate clients, and remind readers of your existence and expertise. The one thing to remember is that there is no such thing as a routine letter. As soon as an organization starts to regard external correspondence as a routine task, it loses its competitive edge.

For the purposes of this chapter, I have divided letter writing into three areas: organization, writing, and format.

ORGANIZATION

1. Before you start to write, think about how your readers will react to the contents of your letter. How will they feel about the message? Will they be happy, indifferent, or upset? This information will affect how you organize your correspondence. Use Worksheet #2 to plan your writing.

2. Routine business letters fall into one of three categories: information, bad news, and persuasion. Each one of these categories has a specific organizational pattern to help you deliver your message. The formats are outlined in Table #5. Examples of each kind of letter are shown in Samples #6 to #15 at the end of the chapter.

WORKSHEET #2
PLANNING TOOL FOR LETTERS

Reader's name

_____

What do you know about the reader? *(his or her background)*

_____

_____

How many times have you already discussed this topic with the reader?

❑ *Never*　　❑ *Once*　　❑ *Twice*　　❑ *More than three times*

What does the reader want to know?

_____

_____

_____

What do you want the reader to know?

_____

_____

_____

What will the reader's reaction be to these points?

❑ *Good news*　　❑ *Mildly interested*
❑ *Indifferent*　　❑ *Bad news*

Based on the reader's reaction, what type of letter will you send?

❑ *Information*　　　❑ *Bad news*　　　❑ *Persuasion*

What do you want the reader to do after he or she is finished reading?

_____

_____

TABLE #5
FORMATS FOR WRITING LETTERS

TYPE OF LETTER		
Information	Bad News	Persuasion
Main idea/ Good news	Neutral idea	Attention-getter
Details	Background information	Introduce the idea, product, or service
	Bad news	Present details
		Benefits to the reader
Call for action	Neutral close	Call for reaction

3. If you are requesting or sending facts, use the information format. It is also called the direct approach because your reason for writing is in the first paragraph.

   This format should be used when you are relaying good news. Remember to jump right in with the good news in the first paragraph. The reader will then pay close attention to the details. The information format is shown in Sample #3.

4. If your reason for writing is to convey unsettling news to the reader, use the bad-news format (see Sample #4). This uses the indirect approach, which means the receiver must read the background information before he or she learns your reason for writing — the bad news. Your reader may

FORMAT FOR INFORMATION LETTER

Dear Mark,

Main idea — Thank you for the information you provided for our home marketing campaign questionnaire. As always, your cooperation has helped ensure the success of this project.

Calling attention to detail — I have enclosed a copy of the findings. Please note that some of this information is extremely sensitive and should be treated as confidential. These sections are marked.

Call for action — We'll be back to request an update in January. Again, Mark, thank you for your continued participation.

Yours sincerely,

---

then be more receptive to the information. If readers are given the bad news first, they might skip the rationale or read it with a biased viewpoint. Remember, it doesn't matter how *you* perceive the message; the important consideration is how your reader will react.

5. The persuasion format is used when you are selling your readers on a product, service, or idea. If you are writing a sales letter, you have only ten seconds to grab your reader's attention. If you don't get it in that time, your reader likely won't finish the letter.

SAMPLE #4
FORMAT FOR BAD-NEWS LETTER

Dear Mr. Brown:

Neutral opening

In response to your letter of May 3, I contacted our national parts headquarters to locate the necessary part for your KV-18943 television.

Presenting facts

It is ABC's policy to always maintain a large stock of repair components for all our products. However, as we produce a wide range of goods, we have had to limit our inventory. We stock parts for a period of ten years after the last manufacturing date of a unit.

Supporting evidence

Your model is over ten years old. We checked with our warehouse in Calgary and, as they did not have the part, asked them to contact their U.S. and Japanese counterparts. We regret that we were not successful in locating the required part.

Bad news

Neutral ending

We trust you enjoyed your last ABC television and that it served you well, Mr. Brown. When the time comes to invest in another television, I recommend that you visit your nearest ABC store at the North Common Shopping Center on Highway 7. I am sure you will be impressed by the knowledge and helpfulness of the salespeople and the wide range of our products.

Sincerely,

Research shows that sales letters of approximately one-and-a-half pages have the best reader response. Half-page letters and those over two pages have a lower response rate. Sample #5 is an example of the persuasion format.

6. Keep your letters short. Tell the reader only what he or she wants and needs to know. Be specific. Use a variety of sentence lengths — the average should be 15 words.

WRITING

7. Watch your opening sentence. Be specific; come to the point. For examples of lively opening lines, see Table #6.

Example We wish to acknowledge receipt of your letter of May 3. *(boring cliché)*

Better I have reviewed the concerns discussed in your letter of May 3.

8. Make each letter an individual talk. Be natural. Use words the reader can easily understand.

9. Emphasize the "you" attitude. Play the reader up, yourself down. Look at the problem from his or her point of view. Try to use *you* early in the sentence rather than *I* or *we*.

10. Whenever possible, avoid using negative words such as *inconvenienced, confused,* or *upset.* This only reminds readers of their earlier states, and they may be beyond this now.

Example We're sorry for any inconvenience that our product may have caused you.

Better Thank you for letting us know about this situation.

11. Reread the rules for tone in chapter 4.

SAMPLE #5
FORMAT FOR PERSUASION LETTER

Begin with a point that the reader can agree with

Dear Ms. Smith:

ABC has always generously supported the Rainbow Ridge General Hospital. Your donation last year of $1,000 was a significant contribution to our 199- campaign.

Introduce the idea

In this time of economic restraint, there is a large gap between available funds and the health care needs of the people of Rainbow Ridge. I am aware that ABC, like several other companies in the community, bases its corporate gift to the hospital on a per employee amount. However,

Present request

we are asking you to rise to the current challenge and increase your donation from last year's $11.17 to $12.94 per employee for 199-.

Details and benefits

The new amount represents the average per employee gift that our top ten Rainbow Ridge companies donate, and it will make a difference to the health of our community members. In addition, your increased contribution will encourage other companies in the area to enlarge their donations.

Call for action

I will call you next week to discuss ABC's contribution to the 199- campaign.

On behalf of the staff of the hospital, who are dedicated to helping the residents of Rainbow Ridge, I would like to send thanks, Ms. Smith, to both you and ABC.

Yours sincerely,

TABLE #6
OPENING LINES

The following opening lines should be used only to jump-start your own creative processes. Think about why you are writing and then come up with your own original opening.

We were pleased to receive your order for 23 lamp shades.

Thank you for sending us one of your motivational lithographs.

Here's the information I promised you last month.

Congratulations! I hear you have just been made king.

I've enclosed the Kingsley Report. It should answer your questions.

I enjoyed meeting you at the COMMIXED exhibit and discussing your future computer plans.

Thank you for talking with me last week regarding your training needs.

Your remarks regarding our new financial package made me re-visit the proposal.

The books you ordered are being shipped today.

Ms. Gloria Dezell suggested I call you regarding…

I'm sorry to hear you are not happy with the conciliation arrangements.

I've read the suggestions in your letter and will review them with my staff.

It's that time again. Our membership year starts April 1.

You've already seen the dramatic difference our professional lawn care can make.

We wish to add our names to the list of those people opposed to…

Welcome to our banking family!

Are you paying too much for…? There are ways to reduce it.

We appreciate your taking the time to inquire about…

On behalf of the…, I would like to congratulate the Credit Valley Hospital for receiving a four-year accreditation.

TABLE #6 — Continued

Thank you for visiting my dealership and allowing my staff to assist you.

You're right. We did make an error.

Thank you for allowing me to introduce you to the many, varied services of ABC productions.

Please make the following adjustments to my account.

Informal openings when omitting a salutation line:

Yes,
  Mr. Smith,
         the posters you require are available for
         immediate shipping.

You are right, Mr. Thomas,
         poor service is not tolerated at Upstairs Downstairs.

We're delighted, Ms. Garrett,
    that you have chosen us to host your Gala Ball.

I need your help...
         Susan

12. In an information or good-news letter, call the reader by name at least once in a one- to two-page letter. Make sure you spell his or her name correctly.

13. Develop your letter step by step. Make it logical. Use connecting words and sub-heads. Keep paragraphs less than ten lines long.

14. Specify definite dates and actions. Don't be vague.

15. Avoid clichés. Refer to Table #3 in chapter 3 for alternatives to common clichés.

16. Always close with a call for action. Let your readers know what you want them to do next — call you, write to you, or wait for you to call them. Sometimes you may not want any action except to understand the information, file it, or think of you in a favorable light. But whatever you want, let the readers know. Table #7 lists closing lines you might use.

| **Example** | If you have any questions, please don't hesitate to contact me. *(Boring cliché)* |
| **Better** | If you have any questions, please call me at (123) 555-7890. |

FORMAT

17. Letters begin with the date and follow with the name and address of the reader. This information is normally typed in upper and lower case; however, some organizations prefer to use only capital letters for the inside address so that it matches the envelope requirements of the postal service (see the examples at Rule #42).

18. If you are sending a letter by fax and then sending the original by mail, make a reference to this fact so that readers will not be confused when they receive the second copy. Type *Sent by fax* or *Via fax* at the left margin under the inside address, or align it with the right margin.

Example	March 1, 199-
	Ms. Helen Smith
	Conference Coordinator
	Humber College
	205 Humber College Boulevard
	Etobicoke, ON M9W 5L7
	Via fax *(if you are not mailing the original, delete this reference line.)*

TABLE #7
CLOSING LINES

I will call you next week after you have had a chance to read the material.

I will call you within the next few days to arrange a convenient time to meet.

I look forward to meeting with you on June 3.

As soon as I receive your check, I will proceed with your registration.

To take advantage of this offer, you must respond by January 30.

We look forward to working with you.

I will call you in mid-March to see how you are progressing.

To complete the report, I need the information by May 30.

All of us at...wish you the very best of the season.

If you would like more information, please let me know. My number is...

Fill in and return the enclosed card, Ms. Smith, and your registration at the conference will be assured.

Looking forward to hearing of your progress.

I will call you next week to further discuss putting my...expertise to work for (company name).

We appreciate the job you are doing for us.

It's a pleasure to have the opportunity to assist you.

I'm sorry we can't be more helpful.

If you haven't sent us your check already, will you please mail it today?

Your reports are usually prompt — what happened this time? We need it immediately.

The check will be in the mail early next month.

Thank you for your patience.

If you need more information, just write to...

(your signature)

If you are sending a one-page letter to a small organization or to someone who sits near a fax machine, you can get away without using a cover sheet. In this case, you might write, *Sent by fax — 2 pages*. Otherwise, use a fax cover sheet. (For more information on fax cover sheets, see chapter 8.)

19. A reference line that includes a file, policy, invoice, or order number may be included for file purposes. This information always appears one to two lines under the date.

Example | March 1, 199-

Reference #17540 - 620499

Ms. Helen Smith
Conference Coordinator
Humber College
205 Humber College Boulevard
Etobicoke, ON   M9W 5L7

20. It is common business practice to use the reader's title of Mr. or Ms. in the inside address and the salutation line. (If a woman prefers to be referred to as Miss or Mrs., she should sign her letters with this title — see Rule #34. It is then the reader's responsibility to ensure that all future correspondence is addressed correctly.) Doctors are addressed as Dr. Brown or as Susan Brown, MD. Do not mix these two styles.

Examples Dear* Mr. Green:
Dear Ms. Blakey:
Dear Dr. Brown:

---

*Some writers don't want to use *Dear* because they feel the reader is not their *dear*. However, this salutation is traditional and many readers would be upset if it were missing from a letter. I have listed a few options in Table #6 that writers might use. These openings can also be used in direct mail, promotional material, and customer service letters. You have to be careful when and where you use them, but I think we will see a lot more of these informal openings in the future.

21. You may omit the *Mr.* and *Ms.* from the inside address and the salutation line if you do not know the sex of the reader and do not have time to find out. The same rule applies if you are unsure of which name is the surname. In these instances, use the reader's full name.

Examples Dear Chris Stone:
Dear R.J. Deakin:
Dear Young Kil:

22. If you do not have a name, address the letter to the position.

Example | March 1, 199-

Human Resources Manager
Business & Industrial Services
Humber College
205 Humber College Boulevard
Etobicoke, ON   M9W 5L7

Dear Human Resources Manager:

23. If you do not have a name or position, omit the salutation line and use a subject line only. Subject lines start at the left margin or are centered on the page. See Sample #6 for an example of this type of letter.

Example | March 1, 199-

Business & Industrial Services
Humber College
205 Humber College Boulevard
Etobicoke, ON   M9W 5L7

Request for Information

September 15, 199-

<u>Recommendation for Timothy Russell</u>

This letter is to recommend Timothy Russell as an outstanding salesperson.

I've known and worked with Tim for more than three years. He is a highly responsible and creative individual. From the day he came to work for us, he was a welcome member of our sales team. He willingly undertook any task assigned him, whether it involved direct sales or not, and his enthusiastic and infectious manner made him popular with all our customers.

I am sorry to lose Tim, but his educational plans call for him to move outside our city. I believe anyone who hires him will be truly fortunate.

Sincerely,

John Watson
Owner

gac

24. Attention lines, and the terms *To Whom It May Concern, Dear Sir/Madam,* or *Ladies and Gentlemen,* are considered old-fashioned and should not be used.

25. Use a colon with a formal salutation: *Dear Ms. Smith:*. Use a comma with an informal salutation: *Dear Robert,*.

26. Some writers use a formal salutation line with *Mr.* or *Ms.* Then, when they are signing the letter, they slash through the name and write the receiver's first name by hand. They believe it gives their letters a personal touch. This technique works with form letters, but is not recommended for normal correspondence. It gives the impression the sender only thought about who the reader was after the letter was written.

Example
> Dear Mr. Redford:

27. The subject line is optional when using a salutation. It usually appears below the salutation and above the first line of the message. The subject line may be introduced by the word *Subject* or some variation of it, or the word may be omitted. The subject line can be placed at the left margin, or centered for emphasis.

Example
> March 1, 199-
>
> Ms. Helen Smith
> Conference Coordinator
> Business & Industrial Services
> Humber College
> 205 Humber College Boulevard
> Etobicoke, ON   M9W 5L7
>
> Dear Ms. Smith:
>
> Subject: Request for information

SUBJECT: FIRST YEAR WARRANTY
PROTECTION
Re: Employment status of William Colgate
Refer to: Policy 657-678
Request for information

28. You may use *I* and *we* in the same letter. *I* means you as an individual. *We* means your whole organization.

29. Remember that opening and closing paragraphs should not exceed six lines. The paragraphs of the body should not exceed ten lines.

30. Make your letter look attractive. Use equal margins with lots of white space.

31. The acceptable closings for today's letters are *Sincerely*, *Yours sincerely*, or *Cordially*. *Regards* is used when writing to a business associate who is also a personal friend.

    Yours truly is used nowadays for more formal writing, such as when writing to ecclesiastical or diplomatic circles.

32. If you are sending a one-page letter on company stationery, it is redundant to include the company name under the complimentary closing. If your letter flows on to a second page without a logo, however, you can add the company name in capitals.

    Example *(nonletterhead paper)*

    Sincerely,
    FIRTH WIDGET COMPANY

    Greg Firth

    Greg Firth
    President

33. The writer's name and title are normally typed four lines below the complimentary closing or the company name. If the letter is short you could leave six lines; if it is long, reduce the space to two lines.

34. Usually a man does not type *Mr.* in his signature, but if he has a name that could be mistaken for a woman's and he wants to ensure that the reader knows who he is, he should use *Mr.* in either his handwritten signature or his typed signature. The same advice holds true for women who want to be referred to as *Mrs.* or *Miss.*

Example

Cordially,

Kris Burton

Mr. Kris Burton
Executive Assistant

Sincerely,

Mr. Kris Burton

Kris Burton
Executive Assistant

35. If a secretary is asked to sign a letter on behalf of the boss, it is now customary for the secretary to sign the boss's name and add his or her initials. An alternative is for the secretary to sign the letter in his or her own name.

Example

Sincerely,

Julia Taush
(m.g.)

Ms. Julia Taush
Marketing Director

Yours sincerely,

Michelle Gutkin

Michelle Gutkin
Secretary to Ms. Taush

36. The typist's initials may be placed at the left margin in upper or lower case. Adding the writer's initials is redundant because the writer's name is already in the signature block. The practice of adding initials is fading as many people now type their own material.

37. If you are including one or more items with your letter, type the word *Enclosure* — or some variation — at the left margin, two lines under the typist's initials, or under the signature block if there is no need for the typist's initials.

Example | Sincerely,

Julia Taush

Ms. Julia Taush
Marketing Director

Enclosure

Examples *(enclosure line variations)*

Enclosure *or* Enclosures
Encl. *or* 2 Encl. or Encl. (2)
Attachment *or* Attachments
Att. *or* 2 Att.

38. Use of the term *c.c.* to indicate other recipients of a letter is under debate. Some people use *c.c.* because it is traditional. Others dislike it because it refers to carbon copies, and they aren't using carbons anymore. Alternatives are to use a single *c* or to spell it out.

No matter which alternative you use, the information is placed at the left margin, two lines below any preceding information.

Example | Sincerely,

Julia Taush

Ms. Julia Taush
Marketing Director

Copy to Paul Becevello *(There is no punctuation as it is on one line.)*

> Copy to: *(Note the use of a colon — a list follows.)*
> Sabrina Anzini
> Paul Becevello
> Greg Firth
> Linda MacKay

39. A postscript, or *PS*, works well with direct mail letters to emphasize a key selling point. However, avoid using a *PS* when preparing normal business correspondence. It can make you look disorganized.

Example *(for a direct mail piece)*

> PS: Remember this offer is valid only until September 30.

The postscript should be typed two to four lines below every other part of the letter, including the *Copy to* and *Enclosure* lines. Leave two spaces between the *PS:* and the first word of the message. The margins should be the same as for the body of the letter.

40. Today most business letters are typed in one of three styles: block, modified block, or modified semi-block.*

In the block style, which is the most common, all parts are aligned with the left margin, including the date, inside address, subject line, text, signature block, and the continuation page heading. The right side is ragged. See Samples #7, #10, and #13.

The modified block style — shown in Samples #8, #11, and #14 — is similar, except the date is centered on the page or placed about five spaces to the left of the center. The complimentary close and the signature block are aligned under the date. The continuation page heading is spread across the top of the page.

---

*To ensure correspondence projects a professional, consistent look to clients and customers, everyone within an organization should use the same layout design. The chosen design should be explained in the company style book and distributed to all employees.

Samples #9, #12, and #15 show the modified semi-block style. Here the first line of each paragraph is indented six spaces. The right side is ragged; the date, complimentary close, and signature block are centered, placed five spaces to the right of the center, or aligned with the right margin. The continuation page heading is spread across the top of the page.

41. If the message continues on to a second page, use a blank second sheet of the same size, color, and texture as the letterhead page. The margins should match. On the top of the second page, type the continuation page heading. This contains the name of the recipient, page number, and date. Do not use abbreviations.

Example *(block style)*

> Page 2
> Ms. Linda MacKay
> August 30, 199-
> Reference Number 23-456-98 (optional)

Example *(modified and modified semi-block style)*

> Ms. Linda MacKay   - 2 -   August 30, 199-
> Reference Number 23-456-98 (optional)

Samples #9, #10, and #14 show two-page letters with continuation page headings in each of the styles.

42. On envelopes, the post office requests all addresses be typed flush left, and written or typed in all capitals with no punctuation marks unless they are part of a place name (e.g., ST. JOHN'S).

Examples MR. COLIN THOMAS
ACCOUNT MANAGER
MICRO-MACROS INC.
323 LAKESHORE ROAD
CRYSTAL CITY SK   K5K 3B3
CANADA (if required)

MR. COLIN THOMAS
ACCOUNTANT MANAGER
MICRO-MACROS INC.
323 LAKESHORE ROAD
CRYSTAL CITY MA   32119-4678
USA (if required)

In Canadian addresses, the two-letter province abbreviation is separated from the postal code by two
spaces.

In American addresses, separate the zip code from the
state abbreviation by two spaces. The zip code may be either
five or nine digits. If the nine digit format is used, there will
be a hyphen between the fifth and sixth digits.

Use the country name only if your letter is being sent
outside your country.

Once you've written and typed your letter, evaluate
it against the points on Checklist #3.

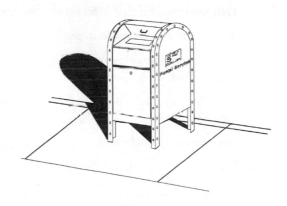

CHECKLIST #3
LETTERS

After you have composed a letter, ask yourself:

☐ Did I think about my reader before I began to write?

☐ Did I analyze the reader's reaction to the message and organize the letter appropriately?

☐ Did I tell my reader what he or she wants and needs to know? Is all other information eliminated?

☐ Does the set-up of the letter meet my company's directives?

☐ Does the page look inviting to read?

☐ Is there plenty of white space and wide margins?

☐ If the letter is longer than one page, did I break up the copy with sub-heads?

☐ Will the opening line interest the reader?

☐ Are all the paragraphs under ten lines?

☐ Are opening and closing paragraphs no longer than four to six lines?

☐ Do any of the details in the body fit into lists? (See Sample #9.)

☐ Are there any clichés?

☐ Did I close with a call for action?

March 1, 199-

Reference number 98 09 123

Sent by fax — 2 pages

Ms. Helen Smith
Conference Coordinator
Business & Industrial Services
Humber College
205 Humber College Boulevard
Etobicoke ON   M9W 5L7

Dear Helen,

Quote for printing brochure

This letter confirms our telephone conversation of February 27, regarding the printing of your publication, *Supervisory Summit*.

The cost of the printing will be $874.89. A specification sheet outlining the cost breakdown is attached.

I have enjoyed working with you on other publications, Helen, and know you will be happy with the quality of this one.

If you send me the rough copy by March 30, I can put it into the following Monday's production schedule so your publication will be ready by April 6. I will call you later this week to confirm the order.

Yours sincerely,

Peter Jansen
Peter Jansen
Printing Coordinator

Att.

March 22, 199-

M.A. SMITH
1243 SPEERS ROAD
NEW YORK NY 99888-1234

Dear M.A. Smith:

Enclosed is the information you requested on CLARITY's Extended Service Plans

As I explained on the phone, the cost of purchasing our Gold Plan, which includes in-home service, would be $137.82 (taxes included).

I understand that you purchased your television from Moonlight TV and Audio on April 17, 198-. Please confirm this purchase by filling in the attached form and returning it to me. Remember to detach the claim form from the registration card, as you will need it for future service.

I look forward to receiving the registration card and your check or money order so I can add your name to our register of satisfied Gold Plan customers.

Sincerely,

Gail Seymour

Gail Seymour
Account Representative

Encl.

September 1, 199-

Ms. Joanne Dearborn
ABC International Trainers
123 Florence Lake Road
Victoria BC   V8V 1A2
Canada

Dear Joanne,

Thank you for your interest in *MJW Communications*. As requested, I am enclosing the information you require for the Asian assignment.

MJW Communications is a business consulting firm that offers workshops and individual consultations to corporations. Our topics include:

- presentation skills
- business writing
- listening skills
- voice projection
- meeting management
- international protocol

Our programs are conducted by a team of facilitators known for their expertise in their particular fields, as well as for the high caliber of their delivery skills. In addition, because our high-content sessions are interactive and highly customized, workshop participants leave the sessions with useful information that can be implemented immediately. Naturally, we offer a money-back satisfaction guarantee.

Page 2   Ms. Joanne Dearborn   September 1, 199-

Joanne, I am confident that *MJW Communications* can meet your needs. I will call you within the week, after you have had a chance to read the attached information. If you wish to reach me in the meantime, please call me at (905) 555-9909.

Sincerely,

Jane Walters

Jane Walters
Principal

Encl.

September 3, 199-

Reference number 034-8961

Mr. Joseph E. Smithers
President, ABC Distributors
18th Floor
125 48th Avenue E.
Seattle WA 12345

Dear Mr. Smithers:

In January of 199-, ABC Distributors signed an agreement
with Rainbow to become the sole distributor of Rainbow's
XXX product line across the United States. Both companies
were pleased with the initial growth pattern and new sales
targets were enthusiastically agreed upon by both parties.

Since December of 199-, however, there has been a dramatic
decline in the sale of our products through your company.
By the end of July, your sales were only $423,000 or 40% of
the goals set for the first half of this fiscal year. And you
have not given us any indication there is hope for improvement over the next few months.

Obviously, part of this can be attributed to the depressed
market. However, our major concern is that since the time
ABC reorganized its management staff, there has not been a
national distribution plan for the sale of our products.

We still believe that a national distributor is the most effective method for Rainbow to build its customer base, and we
hope that our product line complements your product mix
in the business machine marketplace. However, we must establish Rainbow's position in the marketplace, and it is possible that we may be forced to consider other distribution
channels.

Page 2
Mr. J.E. Smithers
September 3, 199-
Reference number 034-8961

I would like to get together within the next two weeks, Mr. Smithers, so that we can discuss specific plans for the future and establish exactly where Rainbow products fit into your company's planning.

I will call you at the end of the week to arrange a time and location.

Sincerely,

James N. Snow
Vice President

jmb

Copy to Susan Blakey

May 1, 199-

Mr. Roy Nelson
Motivational Lithographs Inc.
124 Rogers Road
Crystal City ON L7H 7Y7

Dear Mr. Nelson:

Jean-Luc Boisvertt has asked me to thank you for getting in touch with us regarding your company's motivational lithographs.

Because we strongly believe in creating specifically tailored communications for precisely defined audiences, we do not have a need for such lithographs, although they are truly breathtaking.

Thank you for thinking of us.

Sincerely,

Alexandra Lobach
Alexandra Lobach
Administrative Assistant

SAMPLE #12
BAD-NEWS LETTER
(Modified semi-block style)

February 6, 199-

Mr. S. Leacock
President
Thompson Shipping Inc.
45 Center Street
Austin TX 55577

Dear Mr. Leacock:

Galaxy International and Thompson Shipping Inc. have enjoyed a mutually profitable working relationship for two years now.

Our credit department has recently notified me that over the past three months, Thompson Shipping has billed us for handling charges on shipments to your warehouses.

Although there has never been an agreement between Thompson and Galaxy to pay handling charges, Thompson has deducted $614.78 from our monthly payments to cover this charge. Apparently the additional costs are for services charges and defective products. However, our records show there were no problems with these shipments.

I am sure that this problem is an unfortunate oversight. Please return the $614.78 to Galaxy so that we will not have to reduce your volume incentive rebate by that amount.

I look forward to receiving your check and to many more years of good relations.

Sincerely,

Marion Bradley

Marion Bradley
General Manager

Copy to Margaret Smith
Accounting Department

February 1, 199-

Mr. Donald Therrien
145 Islington Avenue, Unit 6
Fredericton NB E3A 1K9

Dear Mr. Therrien:

If a company is to continue to grow in today's marketplace, it must have great products, provide good service, and listen to its customers.

We at Krypton International pride ourselves on the quality and performance of our products and our customer service. However, we are interested in hearing your experience with Krypton. We know you purchased a camcorder from a Krypton store three months ago. Now that you have had time to use it, we would like to know how you feel about the machine. Would you recommend it to your friends? How do you feel about our sales staff? Were they knowledgeable and helpful?

The attached questionnaire asks 20 simple questions, all related to our products and service. It should take no more than ten minutes to complete. We have even included a pen — yours to keep — to help you get started.

By taking the time to fill in this survey, you will be helping us to assist you in the future with new and improved merchandise and service.

Please return the form to us in the attached, self-addressed envelope. Thank you for your cooperation.

Cordially,

James Ross

James Ross
Customer Service

Encl (3)

April 9, 199-

Ms. Catherine Saito
President
Deluxe Apparel Inc.
1 Park Street
Crystal City MA 32119-4678

Dear Ms. Saito:

If we could cut your production time, increase your sales, and decrease your administrative costs would you be interested

It is true. We can do this and much, much more through computerized information management — a necessity for growing apparel and textile operations.

Supreme, a "Fortune 400" super manufacturer, and Rogers & Jones, a leading developer of software for the sewn products industry, have joined forces to provide computer solutions for the apparel and textile markets.

Rogers & Jones is also recognized throughout the United States and Canada for TABS (Textile Business and Apparel Systems) Software.

The enclosed literature shows how...*(one to two paragraphs on what you want the reader to particularly notice in the brochures).*

Ms. Catherine Saito   - 2 -   April 9, 199-

There are also other solutions we would like to discuss with you personally.

I will telephone you next week to arrange an appointment.

Sincerely,
ROGERS & JONES SOFTWARE

Natalia Lobach
Accounts Manager

3 Encl

October 31, 199-

Ms. A. Tippler
Marketing Manager
ABC Realty
123 Ellerslie Avenue
Miami, FL 33322

Dear Ms. Tippler:

It was a pleasure speaking with you today about our subscription service for Cobden Region, Financial Information Services (FIS).

FIS is a cost-effective monthly publication combining mortgage information with property transaction data. Each monthly edition is comprised of three sections: sales, mortgage registrations, and mortgages coming due. The enclosed flier describes this breakdown in more detail.

The price for each monthly issue is just $150 (plus taxes). For an additional 20% you can also obtain the information on computer disks. If you are planning any mass mailings, the computerized information will simplify the task enormously.

Ms. A. Tippler   -2-   October 31, 199-

FIS will help you increase your business by allowing you to reach hundreds of qualified mortgage prospects every month. Can you afford not to take advantage of this opportunity?

I will call you in a few days, Ms. Tippler, to answer any questions you might have on FIS and on how it can expand your market base.

Cordially,

Jessie Williams
Account Manager

Encl

6

18 TIPS FOR WRITING MEMOS THAT GET READ AND ACTED UPON

Memorandums, or memos, present wonderful opportunities for getting yourself noticed by both colleagues and senior management. They can be used for short internal reports, to give instructions, ask for information, announce a new policy, and update on personnel transfers. In addition, they serve as a permanent record of the decisions made and the actions taken. Unfortunately, readers often consider memos the most boring, useless form of business communication because too many writers use them as a chance to brag about their achievements or as a way to avoid face-to-face meetings. Some writers become lazy and don't ensure their memos are clear, concise, and aimed at the readers' needs. To ensure your memos are read, keep them as short as possible and use every possible technique for good communication:

- Sub-heads to break up long portions of text

- Short paragraphs

- Lists (with numbers, bullets, or dashes)

- White space

As memos are more informal in their organization and tone than letters, they should never be used to send information outside your own company. Businesses that possess electronic mail systems are gradually replacing short memos with e-mails. (For information on how to prepare e-mail memos, refer to chapter 8.) Here are some additional guidelines for the preparation of memos.

ORGANIZATION

1. Think about the information you need to convey. Is a memo the best means of communication? Could the message be delivered better face to face or by phone? If the message is sensitive, think twice before you commit it to a memo. Can you risk having others read this information? How would you feel if your memo were released to the press? In today's world, very little can be kept confidential. If you must document, take care that it cannot be misinterpreted.

   On the other hand, if there are several people who need to receive the information, would a memo be more efficient than a verbal explanation to each of these people? If so, go ahead and write.

   If you are not happy with the quality of your memos, or if you believe you take too much time writing them, try using Worksheet #3 to organize your thoughts.

2. There are four kinds of memos you might have to write. Each kind of memo has its own organizational format, outlined in Table #8.

   (a) The information memo is used to deliver or request information or assistance (see Sample #16).

   (b) The problem-solving memo suggests specific action to improve a situation (see Sample #17).

   (c) The persuasion memo is for occasions when you want to encourage the reader to undertake an action he or she doesn't have to take (see Sample #18).

   (d) The internal proposal memo conveys suggestions to senior management (see Sample #19). Memo reports are discussed in chapter 7.

WORKSHEET #3
PLANNING TOOL FOR MEMOS

1. Fill in the blanks to describe your reason for writing this particular memo.

I am writing to (*supply verb*) _____
(*who*) _____ about
(*what*) _____.

If you have trouble filling in these spaces, the following lists may help you.

Verb (*why you are writing*)	Who (*who will read it*)	What (*what you are writing about*)
inform	my boss	a new idea
persuade	my staff	a new procedure
recommend	colleagues	information
solve a problem	council/board	decision
provide an update	my department	results of a meeting
request	my organization	permission
instruct		a new policy
document		personnel problem
alert		assistance

2. List the key points you must cover in the memo.

_____

_____

_____

_____

3. Record the action you want the reader to take after reading your memo.

_____

_____

4. Now, arrange this information according to the memo formats listed in Table #8, and begin to write.

TABLE #8
FORMATS FOR WRITING MEMOS

TYPE OF MEMO			
Information	**Problem-solving**	**Persuasion**	**Internal Proposal**
Main idea	State the problem	Begin with an agreeable point	Reason for writing
Expand on details	Analyze it	Introduce the idea	Outline present situation and state your proposal
Action required	Make a recommendation	State benefits to the reader	Describe advantage(s)
		Action required	Mention and defuse disadvantage(s)
		Call to action	Call to action

WRITING

3. Follow the rules for good writing listed in chapter 3.

4. Keep your message brief and simple. Specify the actions the reader should take.

5. If you are making a recommendation, don't include only the positive details; include the drawbacks and defuse them yourself (see Sample #19). Otherwise, readers may think you haven't researched the topic thoroughly.

   Example   Although implementing the new system will decrease our productivity for several weeks, the long term benefits of greater accuracy and speed outweigh this concern.

SAMPLE #16
FORMAT FOR INFORMATION MEMO

February 3, 199-

To: Maggie Maloney, Bob Arthur, and Evan Sharp

From: Mark Swierszcz

Re: Planning for September 17-18 Sales Conference

Main idea

It's time to start organizing the annual sales conference again. If the four of us could get together next week, we can begin planning the agenda and dividing the workload. By starting now, the event will be highly successful, and no one will end up handling a lot of last-minute details.

Details

The following is a list of proposed dates and times. Let me know which dates fit your schedule and I will set up a meeting convenient for everyone.

February 11: 9:00–11:30 a.m.
February 12: 1:30–4:00 p.m.
February 13: 8:00–10:30 a.m.

Expected action

Please get back to me by Friday.

FORMAT FOR PROBLEM-SOLVING MEMO

Date: October 24, 199-

To: All Transit Staff (permanent and part-time)

From: Chris Selvam, Transit Planner

Subject: Guidelines for Sharing Workstations

State the problem

Analysis

Some members of the public have complained about receiving inaccurate information from this department regarding bus routes and construction detours. Part of the problem is caused by different shifts sharing the same workstations. If new information is not posted, the next shift is unaware of changes.

Problem

Analysis

A related problem concerns the cleanliness of the workstations. This is particularly true on the weekends when the cleaning staff is unavailable.

Recommendation

To remedy both these concerns, before you leave at the end of your shift please ensure that:

- new information is displayed in an easily accessible spot
- outdated information is removed
- your station is tidy
- all personal hygiene items are removed
- all items borrowed from other workstations are replaced
- your green recycling folder is emptied
- dirty dishes are returned to the cafeteria
- the fridge is emptied

FORMAT FOR PERSUASION MEMO

Date: April 14, 199-

To: All staff

From: Aurora Borealis

Re: Interim Place Annual Campaign

Agreeable point

The staff of Mahood, Rubincam, and Gallant have always had a proud tradition of supporting Interim Place. This is an excellent organization dedicated to providing food and shelter to the needy in our city.

Introduction of idea

Soon, you will be able to share in this fine tradition once again, through your support of the annual campaign.

Benefit to reader

By donating just one hour's pay per month, through payroll deduction, you can help ensure that the human-care needs of our city are met for the upcoming year.

Action required, if reader accepts

Next week, you will receive a payroll deduction form with your paycheck. Please check off your donation and return it to:

Paul McLeod
Payroll Office
5th Floor

Call to action

I urge you to join me in contributing to Interim Place so that together we may help improve the quality of life for the less fortunate.

SAMPLE #19
FORMAT FOR INTERNAL PROPOSAL MEMO

Date: May 4, 199-

To: Todd O'Brien, President

From: Bronwyn McLeod, Administrative
          Manager

Subject: Improving the Appearance of Cobden
          Corp.'s External Correspondence

Reason for writing

It is important that the external correspondence produced by Cobden Corp. reflect the professionalism of our organization. Currently, we do not have a specific style guide. Although all of the staff do use letterhead, they choose whatever font, type size, margins, and letter setup they wish.

Present situation

This individualized approach gives many of our documents an unprofessional — and at times sloppy — appearance. In addition, when several of us are writing to the same client, we do not present the image of a unified group.

Proposal

I recommend that management arrange to have a style guide produced and distributed to all employees. I am sure there is someone on staff who could undertake this project. It should not be a time-consuming process.

Advantages of proposal

Many of our engineers are now typing their own documents, and they have not been trained in standard keyboard practices. This guide will assist them in their work, answer any style questions, and ensure all of Cobden Corp.'s documents have a more professional and consistent appearance.

Disadvantages of proposal and rebuttal	Although our staff are used to "doing their own thing" in terms of correspondence, and some may prefer not to use the style selected, the clients' perception of our company is an important issue. We are trying to build a name for ourselves as an experienced team of hard-working, skilled people. I believe a style guide will contribute to this image.
Call to action	Please let me know if you would like me to assign someone to this task, or if you wish to discuss it further at the weekly meeting.

6. Omit irrelevant words and information. Don't waste readers' time by making them sift through unimportant facts. Not only could this be confusing, but it may provide readers with details suggesting a conclusion or an act you did not intend.

   Ask yourself what the point, sentence, or phrase contributes to the message. If it adds little or nothing, eliminate it.

7. The tone of a memo can range from semi-formal to informal depending on the reader and the occasion. Naturally, a memo to your manager would be more formal than one to a colleague who is also a friend.

FORMAT

8. Memos are used only for written communication within an organization. Therefore, they have a different format than letters. The most common memo starts off with the following information:

   Date:

   To:

   From:

   Subject: *or* Re:

   The exact order of these headings may change depending on the company's official style. Some organizations have letterhead printed in memo form; others provide generic forms to simplify and standardize the information. If your organization does not have a specific form, use the common memo setup.

9. The date is the date the memo is written. Even though this is an informal type of communication, spell out the month. Do not use abbreviations — it makes you look unprofessional. Avoid using numbers for months and days unless this is your company's policy. They can cause confusion.

10. The *To:* and *From:* lines carry the names of the writer and the intended reader. Whether you use *Mr.* or *Ms.* depends on the culture of the organization and the person to whom you are writing. Job titles and department names are often omitted if the sender and receiver know each other well. However, if you believe this memo might serve as a future record, include titles.

    If the memo is sent to more than one person, it may be possible to fit two or three names beside or under the *To* line.

Example   To: Jennifer Becevello, Susan Blakey, and
Shannon McTaggart
or
To: Jennifer Becevello
Susan Blakey
Shannon McTaggart

If it is not possible to fit the names of the addressees in the *To* area, use the phrase: *See distribution list.* At the end of the memo, type the word *Distribution,* leave one line blank, and then list the names of the people who will receive a copy of the memo. Arrange the names by rank, department, or alphabet. (See Sample #20.) If space is tight, use two or more columns.

Be careful who you put on your distribution list. Ensure that the memo goes out to everyone who needs to reads it, but don't over distribute. If someone doesn't need the information or doesn't want it, take them off your list. Don't use a memo merely to blow your own horn. If you have any doubts about whether or not memos should go to a particular person, ask.

11. Include a *Copy to:* line at the bottom of the memo if you want to alert someone to the information but don't expect him or her to carry out the same action as the people listed on the To: line or in the distribution list. Be sure, however, there is a good reason for copying the person. Don't do it merely because you want the reader to think you're a busy employee.

12. Memos should announce their purpose in the *Subject:* or *Re:* line. The subject line should be specific and should instantly give readers enough information to know why they are reading it. It can be two lines long, if required.

Example   New Procedure

Date: July 28, 199-

To: See distribution list

From: Ms. Grace Kiers, Medical Staff Secretary

Re: Ethics Committee Meeting Scheduled for
           September 10, 199-

The first Ethics Committee meeting of the fall season
has been scheduled for Tuesday, September 10, 199-,
at 1600 hours in the hospital boardroom.

A regular monthly meeting time will be decided at
this meeting.

Distribution list

Dr. David Clarkson, Chairperson
Ms. Connie Day, Medical Admin.
Mr. Michael Day, Community Rep.
Dr. Anthony Donohoe, Psychology
Mr. Marc Doucet, Religious Services
Ms. Victoria Glassford, Social Work
Ms. Karen Silverthorn, Nursing
Dr. James Skipper, Surgery
Ms. Jane Watson, Board Rep.
Dr. Lorraine Woolford, Obstetrics
Dr. Michael Zajdman, Pediatrics

Better   New Procedure for Submitting Expense Accounts — Effective Immediately

13. Keep in mind the message should stand by itself and should not rely on the subject line. Do not use the term *above-mentioned*. If you do, the readers' eyes will immediately go back and check the subject line. Then they must come back and find where they left off reading. Don't be lazy. Type out the word or phrase again.

Example   With regard to the above-mentioned project,…

Better   With regard to the Rainbow Ridge project,…

> **Note:** Do not use the phrases *in regards to* or *with regards to*. The correct terms are *in regard to, with regard to, as regards,* or *regarding.*

14. If your reader is not familiar with the subject or with the background of the problem being dealt with, outline it in the opening paragraph. This introduction will provide necessary information months or even years later. The introductory paragraphs in follow-up memos should be shorter and, if necessary, can reference the background information included in the earlier memo.

Example   Here is the May update on the Rainbow Ridge project. (Background information on this project is available in the memo of January 17, 199-.)

15. Use plenty of white space. Remember you have to make the page appear visually attractive so the receiver is encouraged to read it.

16. Include sub-heads to organize the text into manageable bites of information, call attention to key ideas, and signal topic changes. Whenever possible, number points and put series of ideas in a list form.

17. Memos are written communications within an organization. Therefore, they do not have a complimentary close such as *Thank you* or *Thanking you in advance, Yours truly,* or *Sincerely.* Close with the action you wish the reader to take.

Examples   I look forward to your response by July 3.

Please file this information in the Policy and Procedures Manual.

As soon as you send me the figures, I'll complete the proposal.

18. Memos must be signed to indicate they were actually composed by the person listed on the *From:* line. Writers may sign their names in full at the end of the memo or initial their names on the *From:* line. As the name — and the title, if necessary — appears at the top of the memo, it should never be repeated at the bottom.

After you have written your memo, evaluate it using Checklist #4.

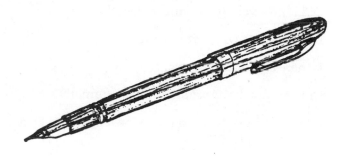

CHECKLIST #4
MEMOS

After you have written a memo, ask yourself:

☐ Did I analyze the reader and his or her needs before I began to write?

☐ Is a memo the best method for communicating my message?

☐ Does the subject line adequately describe the memo's purpose?

☐ Is my tone appropriate to the reader?

☐ Will the reader easily understand the words and jargon I used?

☐ Did I eliminate all unnecessary words and ideas?

☐ Did I keep it as short as possible but include all relevant information?

☐ Did I use a variety of sentence lengths?

☐ Did I use lists whenever possible?

☐ Is there plenty of white space?

☐ Did I follow the appropriate memo format?

☐ If I require specific action from the reader, did I close with this request?

☐ Did I include any necessary dates?

☐ Is this the sort of document I am proud to sign?

☐ Would I be embarrassed if this document were released to the media now or in the future?

7

37 WAYS TO TAKE THE STRESS AND DRUDGERY OUT OF REPORT WRITING AND MAKE YOUR REPORTS READABLE

Reports* play a significant role in business. When you are asked to write one, consider it an investment in your career. After all, anyone who can express new ideas, solutions, and analyses in a clear, concise fashion is always in demand. View your reports as a forum for expression and a chance to shine.

A report is not complicated. It is merely a collection of information, arranged in a particular format, and prepared by an expert. And you, the writer, are the expert.

Does this sound overwhelming? It shouldn't. You communicate orally on the job all the time. A written report is nothing more than an effective summary of the knowledge you have, or the information you can discover, about the area under consideration.

Reports come in a variety of shapes and sizes. They can run anywhere from one page (informal report) to an indefinite number of pages (scientific report). They can be laid out in a variety of formats: memorandum, letter, semi-formal, or formal.

Reports are essential tools for management, especially when they are conceived and prepared properly. Good

---

*Proposals are similar to reports but have a slightly different slant. If you are working on a proposal, this chapter will assist you. However, for a more comprehensive look at this area of business writing, I recommend you read *Winning Proposals* by Hans Tammemagi, published by Self-Counsel Press.

reports give the reader answers, or at least ideas. They are also —

- objective,
- research-based,
- backed by graphics, when possible, and
- written in a clear, concise style.

However, it isn't enough just to provide basic information to your readers and expect them to interpret it. Recipients of reports often claim they are frustrated because reports list information but do not solve problems. Remember, a good report writer gives answers as well as information.

Other complaints associated with reports relate to poor organization of details, weak statements designed to protect the writer, and missed deadlines.

The following tips are designed to help you prepare timely, effective reports that meet the readers' needs.

1. How do you eat an elephant? The answer: one bite at a time. Reports are the same. They can be overwhelming — particularly formal reports. However, if you divide the process into smaller steps, such as the ones listed below, it will ensure your final product is one you can be proud of.

   Here are six steps for successful report writing:

   (a) Analyze the reader and the purpose

   (b) Gather the details

   (c) Organize the information

   (d) Write

   (e) Rest

   (f) Edit and revise

It has been proven that people who spend 40% of their time on the first three stages, 20% on the writing, and 40% on the editing, prepare better reports than people who spend 40% of their report preparation time on the actual writing.

If you are writing draft after draft after draft before you are happy with your report, chances are you are not spending enough time with the analyzing, gathering, and organizing stages.

STEP 1 — ANALYSIS

2. The first step in writing any document is, of course, getting to know your reader. Go back and complete Worksheet #1, Planning Tool for Reader Analysis, in chapter 2.

   You should also identify the secondary audience. The secondary audience consists of people who may be sent copies of your document after the primary readers have reviewed it. For example, your immediate boss requests a report and, after reading it, sends it on to the supervisor, senior management, the board of directors, or council. It may even be made available to the news media and the public.

   Knowing where your report might end up provides a focus for the content, the details to be included or eliminated, and the vocabulary level.

3. In the second step, you should develop a thorough understanding of why the report is needed and exactly what it is you are focusing on. This is an area many writers don't spend enough time on. Until you are clear on the *what* and the *why*, do not begin to write. This information affects the arrangement of the details, and if you haven't determined the *why* and the *what* up front, you will waste time writing and rewriting.

The *why* usually falls into one of two areas. You are either providing information to the readers so they can make a decision or take specific action, or you are analyzing a situation and making a recommendation.

Don't begin writing until you can reduce your purpose statement to two sentences. The statement does not have to be grammatically correct; no one but you will read it. (I like to write the statement on a file card and keep it in front of me while I am working on the report. This keeps me on track and reduces the possibility of detours into irrelevant details.)

Two writers were asked to prepare reports on the maintenance costs of their office's equipment. The manager was thinking of replacing some of the older machines. Each writer worked on a purpose statement and then proceeded with the report. Here are the results:

> **Writer One's purpose statement:**
> The purpose of this report is to assess the maintenance costs of the existing office equipment.

> **Writer Two's purpose statement:**
> The purpose of this report is to present and analyze the maintenance costs of the photocopier, printers, and personal computers in my department and recommend which machines should be replaced. I will also include the costs of replacement equipment and trade-in values.

Writer One spent less time on the purpose statement but a longer time writing the actual text of the report. That report was late and disorganized.

Writer Two spent more time on the purpose statement but less time actually writing. This report was on time and was well received because of the conciseness of the information and the recommendation.

STEP 2 — GATHERING THE DETAILS

4. Once you have focused on the reader and the purpose of the report, it is time to gather the details.* They will come from your own head, hard copy, electronic documents, or from discussions or interviews with concerned sources.

   Remember, effective writers don't collect just the information that interests them. They collect the details their readers need and want.

STEP 3 — ORGANIZING THE INFORMATION

Once the facts have been gathered — and before you begin to write — organize the key points into a logical format.

Short reports

Short or informal reports are one to seven pages in length and are written in letter, memo, or semi-formal format. (A semi-formal report is usually three to five pages in length and has a cover page but none of the other window dressing associated with formal reports.)

5. There are three sections involved in a short report:

   (a) Introduction

   (b) Body

   (c) Conclusion or recommendation

   It is not necessary to present these sections in this exact order. In fact, many readers prefer to have the

---

*Many professional writers use mindmapping techniques at this point to develop a more creative approach to their writing. Other names for similar techniques are brainstorming, clustering, branching, pressure writing, and webbing. They all involve bringing the subconscious mind into the writing process. We don't have room to examine these methods here, but two good books on this subject are *Mindmapping* by Joyce Wycoff and *Writing on Both Sides of the Brain* by Henriette Anne Klauser.

recommendation or conclusion placed near the beginning of the report. In this way, they don't have to read the entire report to obtain the key message. This organizational style for reports is called the direct approach. (See Sample #21.)

The indirect approach, as shown in Sample #22, organizes the report so that the recommendation or conclusion appears at the end. This technique is used by writers when they are unsure how readers will react to their final statements. Some writers believe that if they make their readers wade through the background material, they are more likely to persuade them to adopt the recommendation. This technique does not always work, as more and more readers turn to the final comments first, before reading the report.

6. The introduction should always explain:

   (a) what the topic is,

   (b) why it is being discussed, and

   (c) where the information came from.

   Example   As you requested *(why)*, here is the Historical Homes Committee's report on the deterioration of the city's historic building — The Grange *(what)*. This report is based on our meeting with the tenant who is currently residing at this location *(where the information came from)*.

7. The body explains how the facts lead to the conclusions or recommendations. This section is the most extensive part of the report and can be divided in several ways, as shown in Table #9.

Date: January 12, 199-

To: John Macdonald

From: Charles Tupper

Subject: Plan to Expand the Educational Capability of The Studio

As you suggested, I met with the CPS salespeople, the Systems Group, and the Desktop Publishing Committee to discuss purchasing both a Macintosh and an Amiga computer system for The Studio.

Recommendation
All of the groups felt the addition of the Amiga and the Macintosh computer systems, along with the existing IBM system, would make The Studio a valuable showplace for both end-user training and sales support.

I recommend that we obtain quotes from several companies on the cost of the systems and on the necessary software.

Discussion
The following observations underlie the recommendation:

(a) The explosion of the PC market has opened a whole new world in the area of multimedia applications.

(b) The three main platforms now established in the media marketplace are IBM, Macintosh, and Amiga. Each system's architecture is slightly different.

(c) Computer media have opened new markets for our existing and future products.

(d) We are constantly receiving calls and questions from our own sales reps, dealers, and end-users about how our products interface with the three systems.

(e) The Studio's mandate is to provide end-user training and sales support. It is important that we stay current with the main systems and their applications.

(f) The Studio already has an IBM-based system, which we use for our own production purposes.

October 30, 199-

Ms. Sabrina Anzini
President
Rob Roy Mining Company
5678 McKie Boulevard
Crystal, ON B6B 6X6

Dear Ms. Anzini:

In September 199-, Rob Roy Mining engaged SJL Consultants to carry out an exploration program on the Rainbow Ridge claims in Dulcina Township. The study and a detailed report will be completed in three months' time. However, as you requested, here is an interim report to enable you to proceed with the planning of your on-site activities for the upcoming year.

Exploration program
There are three objectives to this program:

(a) To test two IP low-resistivity zones in the western part of the claim group for sharing and gold mineralizations.

(b) To acquire sufficient assessment credits to keep the claims in good standing.

(c) To collect geological data.

To date, a total of 680.32 meters has been drilled in two holes. The average cost is $62.20 per meter.

Highlights
Some of the highlights of the findings are:

(a) Drill hole B-70 intersected brecciated ultramafics at 500 meters (above sea level).

(b) Gold assays averaged 5.3 grams per ton at 430 to 345 meters (above sea level).

(c) Drill hole B-71 intersected a primarily medium- to coarse-grained dioritic unit at 570 meters (above sea level). No mineralized zones were intersected.

(d) The drill core shows a lithological sequence starting with a mafics to the north, followed by ultramafics, and various phases of a syenitic pluton. The mafics are intruded by a dioritic body or a sill.

Conclusion
Based on the excellent gold showing in drill hole B-70, SJL Consultants recommends that further drilling activities be continued in the Rainbow Ridge claims.

If you have any questions or would like to meet with our on-site team, please call me at (546) 555-6789.

Sincerely,

Paul Becevello
Managing Director

TABLE #9
METHODS OF ORGANIZING REPORTS

Order of importance	List and discuss the most important idea first, then the second most important idea, and so on. The last point is the least important one.
Chronological	Arrange the events being discussed in sequential order, beginning with the first event and continuing on to the last.
Spatial	Describe an object or a process according to its physical arrangement or setting.
Step by step	Instruct the reader on how to carry out a specific activity.
Comparison	Compare items according to specific qualities.

8. If you are preparing an information report for the reader, provide a conclusion. If you are analyzing the information, provide a recommendation.

Formal reports

Formal reports are lengthy, contain complex information, involve research, and are written for upper management or external use.

9. Formal reports are divided into five sections:

  (a) Preliminary parts

     (i) Letter of transmittal

     (ii) Title page

     (iii) Contents page

     (iv) Executive summary or synopsis

  (b) Introduction

  (c) Body

  (d) Conclusions or summary

  (e) Addendums

     (i) Bibliography

     (ii) Appendix material*

     (iii) Index (if required)

10. The letter of transmittal is the letter that accompanies the report. It serves the same purpose as an oral introduction would if you were to deliver the report in person. If the report is prepared for someone within your organization, the letter of transmittal may be written in a memo form.

---

*The appendix contains material that does not fit into the body of the report. It could include a glossary of technical terms, maps, complex mathematical formulas, survey instruments, or questionnaires. Be careful what you choose to include. Do not let this section be a dumping spot for the leftover details.

The letter of transmittal should —

(a) begin with the purpose of the letter,

(b) follow with an overview of the report (if the report includes a separate summary, keep this section brief),

(c) acknowledge those who assisted with the study, and

(d) thank the authority who requested the report for the opportunity to help.

See an example of a letter of transmittal in Sample #23.

11. The title page should be as attractive as possible, as it is usually the first thing the reader sees (see Sample #24). It should include —

(a) the comprehensive title,

(b) the name of the person or authority who requested the report,

(c) the author's name and organization, and

(d) the date submitted.

12. The contents page aids the reader who may want to read only certain parts of the report. It should contain each heading and sub-heading in the report.

If there are more than five graphics in your report, list them in a separate section, titled *List of Figures*, after the contents page. List the name of the figure (table, graph, or chart) and the page number.

13. The executive summary or synopsis is a précis of the entire report. It is the one section you can be assured your audience will read. Keep it short and include only the highlights of the introduction, body, and conclusion or recommendation (see Sample #25).

Although it is one of the first items appearing in the report, you will find it easier if you write this section last.

Dear Mr. Brown:

Here is the report you requested on the need for a central library in the town of Crystal.

To obtain this information, I conducted an opinion survey of 600 area residents. I also met with the staff of the three community libraries in the area to discuss their book collections, staffing, and space requirements.

The study indicates there is a definite need for a central library in Crystal.

The three head librarians and Ms. Marion Seymour of Technical Services were of particular help to me in organizing my research.

Thank you for the opportunity to conduct this study, Mr. Brown. It was both informative and enlightening. Please let me know if you would like to discuss this matter further.

Sincerely,

The comprehensive title

**An Analysis of the High School Drop-out
Patterns of Canadian Students
199-**

The name of the person or authority who requested the report

Prepared for
The Department of Education

The author's name and organization

Prepared by
Julia Taush
and Jeffrey O'Brien
MW Consulting Services

The date submitted

July 12, 199-

Executive summary

On September 23, 199-, Rosehill Realty authorized a study to determine what type of restaurant is best suited for the northwest corner of Main and Sherbourne. This study was prompted by our appraisers, who have determined that this corner property has a best-use value as a location for a restaurant.

The study involved a survey of 500 people who live or work in the area of Main and Sherbourne. This number gives us a sufficient sample to represent the attitudes of the people who may use the restaurant.

The highlights of the study are:

(a) An almost equal number of people favor a restaurant with indoor and outdoor seating, or a fast-food service with indoor and outdoor seating.

(b) Eighty percent of the participants wish to pay less than $8 per lunch.

(c) A large number of participants (78%) spend less than 40 minutes eating lunch.

(d) A significant number of the people interviewed dine out several times a week.

(e) The meal most often eaten in a restaurant by the survey participants is lunch.

Based on these and other findings presented in the report, it is recommended that a fast-food chain, which provides indoor and outdoor seating, be approached to open a restaurant at this location.

Graphics

14. Experts agree that most people get their information visually. Charts, tables, and graphs not only help your reader grasp what you are saying, but they also improve your ability to communicate complex ideas quickly and simply.

15. On the other hand, some people are "chart blind." Give them a chart or a table and they will read all sorts of things into it. According to a 1993 Statistics Canada survey, one in five Canadians has trouble interpreting a line graph. A good tip is to tell people what they are going to see and then present them with the graphics.

   Example   About two-thirds of the staff in our department have been with us for over eight years (see Figure 1).

   Better   As shown in Figure 1, about two thirds of the staff in our department have been with us for over eight years.

   About two-thirds of the staff in our department have been with us for over eight years, as shown in Figure 1.

16. Under no conditions should a graphic be included in the report without being referred to in the text. Ideally, each graphic should come immediately after the text that mentions it. If the illustration is too big to come immediately after the text, it should appear on the page following, unless it is awkward to do so.

17. To avoid confusion, call each table, chart, or graph a *figure*, and number them sequentially. Don't forget to give each graphic a comprehensive title.

18. Once you have analyzed your reader, gathered the data, and picked the organizational pattern, fill in a storyboard planning sheet. Worksheet #4 is my favorite layout, but it can be easily modified to fit the needs of your specific report.

    These storyboard sheets are also beneficial when preparing a team report. Each member of the team fills in and works on the relevant portions of the sheet, and the group manager knows what to expect from every writer.

19. Seven is the magic number for writing reports. Never have more than seven main points. This is the limit for a reader's attention span. Likewise, never include more than seven sub-points for a main point. You may even go a level deeper into the report — to sub-sub points — but any level lower than that will only detract from the main points.

20. One of the major complaints about reports — from readers and writers — is that they are often not as well written as they should be because they are prepared under time constraints. To avoid a poorly written, or late, report, plan out your writing time before you start, working backwards from your due date.

    Worksheet #5 is a time sheet designed for writing reports. On the top line, record the various steps you need to take to prepare your report. In the left margin, record the various parts of the report. Then record the dates on which you intend to accomplish the specific areas. In the bottom of the boxes, fill in the dates when you actually complete that step. Now you can easily see how you are progressing, and will know when you can relax or when you have to step up the pace. Sample #26 shows this time sheet filled in for writing this book.

WORKSHEET #4
STORYBOARD PLANNING TOOL FOR REPORTS

REPORT TITLE _____

FINAL DEADLINE _____

SECTION REQUIREMENTS

Point 1 _____

    Sub-point _____

    _____

    _____

    Graphic requirements _____
    Appendix requirements _____

Point 2 _____

    Sub-point _____

    _____

    _____

    Graphic requirements _____
    Appendix requirements _____

Point 3 _____

    Sub-point _____

    _____

    _____

    Graphic requirements _____
    Appendix requirements _____

Point 4 _____

    Sub-point _____

    _____

    _____

    Graphic requirements _____
    Appendix requirements _____

WORKSHEET #5
TIME SHEET

	Organize ideas	Write first draft	Edit first draft	Write second edit	Final edit

SAMPLE #26
TIME SHEET

	Organize ideas	Write first draft	Edit first draft	Write second edit	Final edit
Preface	Aug 31 / Aug 31	Aug 31 / Aug 31	Sept 5 / Sept 5	Sept 6 / Sept 6	Oct 7 / Oct 9
Chpt 1 Writing	Aug 16 / Aug 16	Aug 16 / Aug 16	Aug 17 / Aug 17	Aug 18 / Aug 18	Sept 20 / Sept 20
Chpt 2 Readers	Aug 21 / Aug 21	Aug 22 / Aug 21	Aug 29 / Aug 29	Aug 30 / Aug 30	Sept 21 / Sept 20
Chpt 3 Rules	June 30 / June 30	July 7 / July 6	July 12 / July 12	July 17 / July 13	Sept 22 / Sept 21
Chpt 4 Tone	July 17 / July 17	July 19 / July 19	July 20 / July 20	July 21 / July 22	Sept 25 / Sept 25
Chpt 5 Letters	July 24 / July 24	July 26 / July 26	July 27 / July 27	July 28 / July 28	Sept 30 / Sept 27
Chpt 6 Memos	July 31 / July 30	Aug 2 / Aug 1	Aug 3 / Aug 3	Aug 4 / Aug 4	Oct 2 / Oct 2
Chpt 7 Reports	Aug 8 / Aug 8	Aug 8 / Aug 8	Aug 10 / Aug 10	Aug 12 / Aug 12	Oct 3 / Oct 3
Chpt 8 Faxes and e-mail	Sept 6 / Sept 6	Sept 7 / Sept 7	Sept 8 / Sept 8	Sept 9 / Sept 13	Oct 5 / Oct 5
Chpt 9 Writing	Aug 14 / Aug 14	Aug 15 / Aug 15	Aug 17 / Aug 17	Aug 18 / Aug 18	Oct 6 / Oct 6

STEP 4 — WRITING

21. When you are writing lengthy reports, you don't have to start at the beginning and work through to the end. If you have completed your storyboard sheet, you can start at any point you wish. Some people prefer to begin with the easiest sections and warm up to the harder ones. Others start with the most difficult.

22. Follow the normal rules for business writing discussed in chapter 4.

23. Short reports may be written in point form. Formal reports should be written with complete sentences, paragraphs, and headings.

    You can use a point-form style when dealing with —

    • an existing client who does not require extensive background information,

    • one reader who does not have any personal style issues, or

    • information you want to deliver in a casual manner.

    Use full-length sentences when several people with different information needs will read the document.

24. Long paragraphs give the impression that the ideas expressed are important; short paragraphs imply lesser thoughts. However, too many long paragraphs may intimidate some readers, as they call for more concentration. Try to reduce the number of paragraphs over ten lines in length.

25. Visual appeal is important in reports. Make sure you have plenty of white space, and leave ample margins in case the report is bound or placed in a binder. Some writers leave a wider margin on the right-hand side so readers can add their comments or questions in the appropriate places.

26. The tone in formal reports is objective and formal. Avoid the first person (*I* or *me*), and use more passive voice sentences than you would for letters, memos, and short reports.

27. Be prepared to make strong statements. Don't hedge when you take a stand; it makes you appear unprofessional and frustrates your readers.

    Example Based on these figures, which I hope are accurate, it is recommended that bidding be considered for the purchase of ABC company.

    Better Based on these figures, I recommend that Crystal Corporation purchase the ABC company.

28. Use the passive voice when presenting negative findings.

    Example You lowered morale in the office when you announced five people would be laid off.

    Better Morale in the office lowered when it was announced five people would be laid off.

29. Use active voice sentences when making recommendations.

    Example It is recommended that the new XYZ software package be purchased by the department.

    Better We recommend the department purchase the new XYZ software package.

30. If comparing two or more items, discuss them by the qualities being measured rather than by the items themselves (see Table #10).

31. Research shows that, with a long report, almost all readers will review the executive summary, a majority will read the introduction because it comes next, and then some will flip ahead and read the conclusion. Few will

TABLE #10
ORGANIZATION FOR COMPARATIVE REPORTS

Example	Better
Introduction	*Introduction*
Site A Condition of existing 　buildings Parking Costs	*Condition of existing buildings* Site A Site B Site C
Site B Condition of existing 　buildings Parking Costs	*Parking* Site A Site B Site C
Site C Condition of existing 　buildings Parking Costs	*Costs* Site A Site B Site C
Recommendation	*Recommendation*
This method forces readers to flip back and forth between pages to understand the comparison.	This method presents the information in a format that is easier for the reader to evaluate.

read the entire body of the report. Therefore, following Rules #32, #33, and #34 is essential.

32. In a long report, all major points should appear three times: in the body, in the executive summary, and in either the introduction or the conclusion or recommendation. Remember, few readers read a long report from cover to cover. By recording key points three times, there is a better chance that your audience will read those particular points.

33. Always reread the introduction after you have finished the entire report and make any necessary changes. Sometimes, in writing the body — even though you follow the outline you created before you began to write — you may add some extra details or take a slightly different slant than the one initially planned.

    Make sure the introduction presents a concise picture of what is to follow. If it doesn't accurately reflect the upcoming ideas, your readers will be annoyed.

34. Use descriptive sub-heads to deliver information to your readers. Keep in mind today's busy readers. Many will not take the time to thoroughly read a lengthy report, but they will skim the heads and sub-heads. Ensure that these titles are comprehensive and that they explain the gist of the information that follows.

    Example   By-elections

    Better   Rising costs of by-elections

35. In a long report, use a recognized numbering system and stick to it. Table #11 shows three basic systems you could use for your reports.

TABLE #11
NUMBERING SYSTEMS FOR REPORTS

Roman numeral	Alphanumeric	Decimal
I. (main point)	A.	1.0
A. (sub-point)	1.	1.1
1. (sub-sub point)	a.	1.1.1
2.	b.	1.1.2
B.	2.	1.2
II.	B.	2.0

STEP 5 — RESTING

36. Research indicates that writers do a better editing job if they rest at least two hours before beginning to edit their own writing. (Twenty-four hours is even better.) That way, you will be looking at the material with a slightly fresher, more objective, eye.

Don't forget to rest.

STEP 6 — EDITING

37. Editing is the key to all good reports. Forty percent of the report process should be spent in this stage. And remember to do a spell check both manually and electronically. Checklist #5 gives you some questions to ask yourself.

CHECKLIST #5
EDITING REPORTS

After you have written your report, ask yourself:

- [ ] Does the title adequately describe the purpose of the report?

- [ ] If I have written a formal report, does the executive summary carry the significant highlights without overwhelming the reader with details?

- [ ] Does the introduction explain the purpose of the report?

- [ ] If it is a long report, are all major points discussed three times in the appropriate sections?

- [ ] Did I include all the information the reader has to and wants to know? Did I omit everything else?

- [ ] Is the information arranged in a logical order?

- [ ] Are the figures, names, and dates accurate?

- [ ] Did I use the passive voice for negative findings and the active voice for recommendations?

- [ ] Is my report visually appealing?

- [ ] If my audience reads only the headings and sub-headings, will they understand the gist of the report?

- [ ] Did I use a vocabulary level my readers will understand? My secondary readers?

- [ ] Did I write sentences under 40 words that require no more than four pieces of punctuation?

- [ ] Are a majority of the paragraphs less than ten lines long?

- [ ] Did I use lists when possible?

- [ ] Is the numbering system consistent?

- [ ] Did I use connecting words and phrases to move the reader through the material?

- [ ] Did I check for grammar errors or misused words?

8

21 THINGS YOU NEVER LEARNED IN KINDERGARTEN— FAXES AND E-MAIL

With today's electronic communication tools we have truly become a global village, bound together by miles of copper and fiber cables, satellite links, and telephone lines. Furthermore, some of these tools — including e-mails and faxes — have changed the pace of business forever.

People respond faster to e-mails or faxes than they do to correspondence sent by regular mail. The response is even faster with a phone call, but in our hectic world you often end up on a voice mail system. In addition, e-mail eliminates the inaccuracies caused by muddled spoken messages, and it leaves an information trail.

However, there are some downsides. Faxes and e-mails —

- do not operate in real time. The writer has no control over when the receiver will read the message.

- are like postcards. They have some degree of security, but the possibility exists that they will be read by others without your knowing about it. Therefore, faxes or e-mail should never be used for confidential or sensitive information.

The cost of sending a fax is equal to the cost of a phone call. Internet e-mails are even cheaper to send than faxes because all e-mail addresses are the same distance from each other, whether you are communicating with someone in London, England, or London, Canada.

Most large companies do not realize what they pay each year to send faxes. A 1993 Gallup study found that the average large Canadian company spends slightly over $2 million a year on fax traffic. This figure is based on the cost of the phone calls, and doesn't include the cost of the machines or the paper. Although this expense could be reduced by making use of special fax-machine features that permit faxes to be sent at night, when long-distance telephone rates are cheaper, few companies take advantage of this option.

Currently, it is easier to send drawings, maps, and photos by fax than it is to attach them to e-mails. However, this will change as more offices gain access to scanners and as new standards evolve on the Internet.

FAXES

Faxes should be prepared with the same care you would use in writing a letter. Keep your fax as brief as possible — a long fax diminishes its sense of urgency — and watch out for spelling and grammar errors. Remember your image! Here are a few guidelines for preparing faxes:

1. When sending a fax to a large organization, always include a cover sheet containing the name of the sender, his or her fax and phone numbers, the number of pages being sent, and a phone number to call in case there is trouble receiving the fax (see Sample #27). There are several software packages on the market today that can help you design a template for your cover sheet.

   When faxing a letter — prepared on letterhead and containing the sender's full address — to a small business, there is no need to attach a cover sheet, as there should be no doubt at the receiving end who the fax is directed to.

DATE: September 28, 199-

FROM: J Watson & Associates
             4041 Powderhorn Court
             Mississauga, ON L5L 3C3 Canada
             Fax: 905-820-9246 Tel: 905-820-9909

TO: Warren Evans
             The Service Excellence Group
             Fax: 905-858-0099 Tel: 905-877-0624

MESSAGE:

             Warren,

             Here's the information I promised on the
             ABC account.

                        Jane

"ADVANCING BUSINESS COMMUNICATIONS"

Number of pages, including this one ___3___

2. When you use a cover sheet, ensure that it has an appropriate design. A good cover sheet includes a logo or slogan that reproduces clearly on fax paper, giving you another opportunity to reinforce the identity of your company. Don't use your regular letterhead if it has embossing or metallic type; these devices won't reproduce effectively by fax. If you are in doubt about the quality of your faxes, send one to yourself and check the results.

   People who are running small businesses often purchase books of cartoon-type fax cover sheets. These can be amusing to the reader, but make sure they don't detract from your message.

3. Check the appearance of your fax. Make sure there is a margin of at least three-quarters of an inch so words will not get cut off. You should use a sans serif typeface, such as Helvetica, set at 12 point so the fax is readable.

4. Proofread. Faxes are legally binding documents. If you quote a price or send contractual information, make sure it is accurate.

5. Type your message. Documents are not always as clear as the original when faxed; a fax written in pen could be difficult to read.

E-MAILS

E-mails, whether they are transmitted through a corporate electronic network or via the Internet, are a quick, convenient, and relatively inexpensive way to send and receive messages. E-mails decrease the time information spends in limbo — the time after the message has been sent, before it is received — and, when used responsibly, boost efficiency and productivity.

   However, some users do abuse e-mails by stuffing them with personal messages, trivia, jokes, or solicitations. One employee voiced his concerns about the company's annual Christmas party to a senior manager through the corporation's e-mail network and — accidentally, he claimed — copied everyone working for the company. By using the "all employees" distribution list, he jammed the message system for several hours during peak working time. The company was not amused.

Other users fail to read their messages, canceling the speed advantage of e-mail. Or they forget to purge old messages, consuming disk space with useless information and causing headaches for the computer systems department.

Some senders write long, windy messages with the important elements buried somewhere in the third screen. And some neophytes believe that because e-mail is a speedy, internal message service, they can ignore spelling, punctuation, and grammar. Wrong!

Despite its brevity and informal tone, e-mail is still more like writing than speaking and should be handled as such. Before putting your fingers to the keyboard, think about what your reader needs to know. Write a quick draft and then edit and proofread it. Remember, an e-mail can be printed and you can be held responsible for the information given.

Here are some other general rules:

6. E-mails are more informal than other forms of writing. Don't use a full name and title in the message if this information is automatically included in the address area.

Start with the person's first name, or if you are writing to a group of people, begin with the word *Greetings*.

Example   Greg,
I am going to need the figures for the Johnson contract by noon tomorrow.

Example   Greetings,
I have set a meeting with our planning committee and the building group for Thursday, March 24, at 10:00.
Place — Administration Boardroom.
Call me if you can't make it.

7. Use a meaningful subject line. Remember, the people receiving the message may receive numerous messages every day. To encourage them to read yours, provide a subject line that is interesting and relevant.

8. Keep paragraphs short, nothing longer than five lines. Use lists to break up ideas. And don't right-justify. If your message is lengthy, forget e-mail and send a memo by fax or internal mail. (Computer screens are harder to read than the printed page. E-mail is not an appropriate medium for long messages or messages with multiple attachments.)

9. Use correct punctuation — your message will be easier to interpret — and capitalize appropriate letters. If you use all capital letters, it will look as if you are yelling at the receiver.

10. Realize that humor and emotions can be lost or misinterpreted in e-mail, just as they are in letter writing, so be careful how you phrase your message. Sometimes an extra sentence or two will reduce the abruptness of your words.

Some users have developed a new art form called *smileys* to show their feelings. Smileys are also called *emotions* or *glyphs*. A smiley is a set of symbols that, when turned on its side, represents an emotion. Here are a few:

:)	happy	:-7	skeptical
:(	sad	:D	laugh
;-)	sarcastic	:-O	oh, oh!

Example   Ruth,
         Sorry, but the manuscript will be
         one week late. :(
         Suzanne

11. Keep your message simple and straightforward. Remember the words of courtesy: *please* and *thank you*.

12. If you have an urgent deadline, include it in both the subject line and the body.

   Example *(subject line)*
         Information for Alliance Contract

   Better   Information for Alliance Contract Required for Sept. 6

   Example *(body)*
         Thanking you in advance for your cooperation.

   Better   I appreciate your sending me the information by September 6 so I can include it in the proposal.

13. Never chew anyone out on-line. If you feel you must tell someone off, wait until both of you have cooled off and then discuss the issue by phone. Don't ever respond to a message when you are mad!

14. When sending an e-mail message, it's easy to send copies to a lot of people; be careful of this practice. Don't send copies of your message to everybody in the world unless you know they want or need to receive it.

15. Some e-mail software packages automatically repeat the original message in your response. This is great for

reminding the recipient what his or her message was about. However, edit the original message down so you leave only the relevant text, not a long original message. As well, some e-mail packages allow you to turn off the feature of repeating the original message.

16. If you have a problem you want an answer for, provide enough detail for experts to work with. Explain the problem, what solutions you have already tried, and the results. If the problem involves error codes on your computer, cut and paste the actual code into your message.

17. Whenever possible, copy and paste material into your e-mail rather than including an attachment. Busy people do not always bother to open their attachments.

18. Never e-mail anything you would not care to see on the front page of the newspaper. Permanently purging an e-mail from your system is not as easy as it seems. Deleting an item does not necessarily erase the contents from your hard drive.

19. Always consider your readers before sending an e-mail. What do they want to know and what do they need to know? Omit everything else.

20. Don't stop the task you are working on every time you get a new message.

21. Check your messages at regular intervals and delete all unnecessary messages.

After you have composed an e-mail, examine it against Checklist #6 to make sure you haven't forgotten anything.

CHECKLIST #6
E-MAILS

After you have composed your e-mail, ask yourself:

☐ Did I think about my reader before I composed the message?

☐ Is an e-mail the right method for communicating this particular message?

☐ Is the subject line descriptive and interesting?

☐ Is there a deadline involved? Did I include this information in the subject line and in the body?

☐ Did I include only the pertinent details and omit everything else?

☐ Is the material organized in an easy-to-follow manner?

☐ Did I keep the paragraphs short — under five lines in the body and two to three lines in the opening and closing paragraphs?

☐ Did I use lists to convey a series of ideas?

☐ Are the names, dates, times, and figures accurate?

☐ Did I type the message in upper and lower case, and use the correct punctuation?

☐ Have I allowed the right side of the type to run ragged?

☐ Are there any spelling errors?

☐ Does the closing line tell the readers what they are to do next?

☐ Did I try to reduce the number of attachments?

☐ Am I sending this message only to the people who need to receive it?

9

42 SUGGESTIONS TO WRITE FASTER, AVOID WRITER'S BLOCK, COACH OTHER WRITERS, AND BECOME AN EFFECTIVE GHOSTWRITER

This chapter consists of leftovers — the writing tips I have found helpful but which really don't fit into one specific spot. This is not to say that this information isn't important. In fact, most of these techniques can be used in handling any writing assignment.

WRITING FASTER

You've been given a writing assignment — a major report for your company, or an important letter — and you've developed a case of stage fright. You just can't get started, you can't focus your thoughts, and the words won't come. You despair of completing the assignment on time.

If so, the following section is especially for you. It helps you establish a writing routine, and describes games to trick your mind over the hesitation.

1. I find that writing is like holding a tangled ball of string in your hand. All the ideas, facts, questions, and answers are wrapped together, and you have to keep pulling and poking at them — designing purpose statements, working with scratch pads, and preparing outlines — until everything suddenly unravels and the words pour forth. To try to start writing any earlier is a waste of time.

2. Select a good writing environment. Everyone requires something different. Some people can work only if they are surrounded by silence; others need noise or music. Some writers want to be able to stare out a window; others are happy only if their desks are completely clear of clutter. It doesn't matter; just determine what works for you.

3. Choose the appropriate tools or props. I have heard of one man who is more productive if he writes his reports standing up at a drafting table. A close friend has a hat she puts on when she wants to write. This is to remind herself and her colleagues that writing is the task she is concentrating on. A former coworker could work only if he had a large cup of coffee beside him. Have you identified your prop?

4. The time of day is important. We all have different body rhythms. This means we perform different tasks better at some times of the day than others. Many young people, who have been out of school for just a few years, claim their most productive writing time is late in the day. Older business people usually find their most productive time is first thing in the morning. Determine your best writing time and arrange your day so you work on important writing assignments during this period.

5. Set aside relatively large blocks of uninterrupted time in which to do your writing. Obviously one hour of uninterrupted time is better than three hours of interruptions. This suggestion is easy to follow if you have an office and can shut the door and turn off the phone, or if you have the luxury of working from home. However, if you are in an open office, you have a problem. The best I can suggest is to put a small sign in your workspace, stating that you are working on a report and asking not to be disturbed until a specific time. You can also notify your coworkers of this needed time-out.

6. When you receive a writing assignment, immediately organize your schedule to allow plenty of time for preparation, writing, rewriting, and editing. Leaving it too late means you won't have adequate time to perform all these tasks, and your report will not be as effective as it should be. Remember, again, the old tongue-in-cheek advice on how to eat an elephant — one bite at a time. Break the writing task into small, easy-to-digest steps.

   Also plan for adequate "simmering" time between the steps. This ensures you are continually examining the project with a relatively fresh eye.

Plan for adequate "simmering" time between steps.

7. Once you have identified the key points to be included in your report, you don't have to begin at the beginning and work your way straight through. You could begin at an easy section or a hard one. If you are waiting for research to be completed on one portion, begin writing another area.

8. Before writing, re-read your notes and outline. Then take a few minutes' break. Do something completely different for at least ten minutes. Come back and begin to write as fast as you can. Don't stop to edit or consult your notes. After you have finished the section, check your notes for any point you may have forgotten. Then edit for spelling, grammar, and visual appeal.

9. Do not write and edit at the same time. Too many business people start writing, and when they come to a word they're not happy with, they stop and check their thesaurus for a better one. Or if a sentence isn't perfect, they stop and rework it. This is wasting time.

The different workings of the right and left sides of our brains are now common knowledge. The right brain handles the actual writing process. The left brain is responsible for spelling, grammar, and editing. When you pause to search for the best phrase or sentence, you halt the right brain's activities and let the left brain take over. What would happen if you tried to drive a car with your feet on the brake and the gas pedal at the same time? The ride would be jerky and your progress slow. Why operate your brain this way? When you write and edit at the same time, you only slow yourself down.

Remember the golden rule for writers:

> **First write it; then make it right.**

10. If you have to stop before you have finished the entire writing phase — because the project is too long to complete in that sitting, or because it is time to go to a meeting or lunch or home — be careful where you leave off. If you complete an entire section, when you come back to write you will have to reread much of the previous material before you can get started. However, if you quit in the middle of a sentence in the middle of a paragraph in the middle of a section, you'll find it easier to resume writing in the future. Just reread the sentence and fill in the missing information. This should lead you into the next sentence and so forth. This is a very simple, effective technique, but it is surprisingly hard to do.

11. Another technique, if you have to call it a day before finishing the project, is to leave yourself notes for the next day's work.

12. Divide the editing stage into three phases. First, review the material to determine if all the important details have been included or if any points need further explanation. Second, check the material for style, grammar, spelling, and punctuation. Third, look at the appearance. Is there plenty of white space? Does it look easy to read?

13. Read your draft aloud. Put a pencil check wherever you stumble, but don't stop reading. When you have finished, go back to the marked sections. These are the areas you have to improve.

14. Some people can go for weeks in their jobs and not have to write anything more than a few short e-mails. Keep your writing "muscles" in shape. Read and edit everything you can get your hands on. It will prepare you for your next writing challenge.

15. Maintain a file of correspondence and reports you think are particularly well written. These documents may serve as future references for layout and organization.

16. The best way to become a good writer is to write and write and write.

AVOIDING WRITER'S BLOCK

Sometimes, no matter how hard you push, the words and ideas just won't come. This happens to all writers at some point. Here are some ideas to break through the barrier.

17. Let it go. Move away from the keyboard and do something else, preferably something that doesn't involve creative thinking. Make some sales calls, organize your desk or files, make photocopies, or run errands. After a

minimum of one hour — preferably two — turn back to the keyboard and the ideas should flow. Your brain has had a chance to recharge.

18. Write a letter. Take the details you are wrestling with and explain them in a letter to a close friend.

19. Imagine you are talking on the phone. How would you explain this important message to the listener?

20. Start with a purpose sentence. Begin by writing *The purpose of this* (letter, memo, or report) *is to*…and then add *why*.

21. Open a dictionary at random and choose a word. Use this word in the first sentence in your document.

22. Write badly and then leave the material for a day. Hopefully, you will find something salvageable in it when you come back to it.

23. Try writing with colored markers on legal-size paper, or on paper that is even larger.

24. Dictate your thoughts into a tape recorder.

25. Don't edit and write at the same time (see Rule #9).

26. Relax. This, of course, is easier for people working at home. Meditate. Read a book. Perform some deep breathing exercises.

27. Get some exercise. Go for a walk, play a game of squash or racquetball. This remedy is often the most effective. It chases away the cobwebs, gets the blood flowing, and releases creative energies.

HELPING OTHERS IMPROVE THEIR WRITING

Helping others improve their writing is not an easy task. If you continually make major revisions to your employees' work, chances are they will give up trying to improve. "After all, why bother?" they'll say. "The boss will only rewrite it."

On the other hand, if you overlook vague or poorly written correspondence, it will reflect badly on your department and organization.

Here are some guidelines to help you coach your staff in preparing well-written documents.

28. First, ensure your own writing reflects today's business writing style: clear, concise, and courteous.

29. Understand the differences between editing, rewriting, and revising. If you are editing, your job is to improve the clarity, accuracy, and effectiveness of the material. The changes are minor, and you could make the alterations without consulting the author.

    When you revise, you indicate the changes required in the sentence structure, tone, organization, and the inclusion or elimination of details. Then you pass it back to the author so he or she can rewrite the material. This is a good learning process for the author, but can be time-consuming.

    Rewriting is when you make the changes yourself instead of letting the author make them. This is faster, but the writer will not learn from the experience.

30. Don't attempt to edit someone else's work when you are in a bad mood. When you are angry or upset, your judgment is off and you will end up revising material that at another time would be acceptable.

31. Choose a comprehensive style and grammar book that is available to everyone in the office.

32. Don't use a red pen when correcting someone's work. It makes people feel they are back in school.

33. Change words only if they are incorrect or fuzzy. Don't change words because they aren't your favorite words.

34. Never rewrite an entire paragraph. Mark it for the author to revise.

35. Don't write cryptic words, such as *confusing* or *awkward*, in the margin. Comment on why the passage isn't working.

36. If a problem appears repeatedly, number your comments and refer to the number when the problem appears again, rather than rewriting your concerns.

37. Circulate well-written reports so that staff have a standard to go by.

38. Praise your staff — preferably in public — whenever they prepare a well-written document.

BEING A GHOSTWRITER

Being asked to write a letter or memo for someone else's signature is not uncommon in the business world. Perhaps the signer is busy, or perhaps you have more background or insight into the situation than he or she does. In any case, ghostwriting can be tricky. Signers want documents to match their own writing styles.

39. After you have considered the reader and the details that must be included, analyze the signer's normal style and then temporarily adopt it.

Does the signer:

- Begin with a pompous opening or a reference to the reader?

- Use a friendly or pompous note?

- Favor the pronoun: *I, you, we,* or *it?*

- Arrange series of ideas in lists?

- Prefer long or short paragraphs and sentences?
- Have any favorite words?
- Use the active voice more than the passive voice?
- Use contractions such as *it's* and *can't*, or spell words out in full?
- Close with a refreshing ending or a cliché?

40. The signer's personality usually shows more in the beginning and end than in the body, so match the signer's normal opening and closing lines as much as possible.

41. Do not be upset when, after you have worked hard to adopt the signer's style, he or she still makes changes. This is to be expected. Most signers feel they must make some alteration to the document in order to claim some authorship.

    However, do not complete ghostwriting assignments in a careless manner because you expect signers to revise them. This will only make you look incapable and unprofessional.

42. If a signer's style is completely outdated, you are not going to be able to change him or her overnight. You are going to have to compromise. Hopefully, you will find a middle-of-the-road style you both can live with.

BIBLIOGRAPHY

Brill, Laura. *Business Writing Quick and Easy*. New York: AMACOM, 1989.

Canadian Press. *The Canadian Press Stylebook*. Toronto: Canadian Press, 1993.

Carroll, David L. *A Manual of Writer's Tricks*. New York: Marlowe & Company, 1995.

Klauser, Henriette Anne. *Writing on Both Sides of the Brain*. San Francisco: HarperCollins, 1987.

Pywell, Sharon L. *Writing That Works*. Burr Bridge: Business One Irwin/Mirror Press, 1994.

Sabin, William A. and Sheila O'Neill. *The Greg Reference Manual*, 3rd Canadian ed. Toronto: McGraw-Hill Ryerson, 1986.

Soden, Garrett. *Looking Good on Paper*. New York: AMACOM, 1995.

Strunk, William, Jr. and E.B. White. *The Elements of Style*, 3rd ed. Toronto: McGraw-Hill, 1979.

Tammemagi, Hans. *Winning Proposals*. Vancouver: Self-Counsel Press, 1995.

Venolia, Jan. *Write Right!* Vancouver: Self-Counsel Press, 1995.

Vik, Gretchen N. and Jeannette Wortman Gildsdorf. *Business Communication*. Burr Bridge: Richard D. Irwin, 1994.

Wycoff, Joyce. *Mindmapping*, New York: Berkley Books, 1991.

INDEX